PENNINGTON

POSITIVE

PARENTING

Dr. Yvonne Pennington,
Mother of Wynn and Ty Pennington,
Offers her Parenting Workbook for
Managing Children Positively
(Even if One Has ADHD)

This book is dedicated to my wonderful sons and the thousands of parents who have attended my *Pennington Positive Parenting* workshop for thirty six years. Without all of you this book would not have come to fruition.

Copyright © 2007 Dr. A. Yvonne V. Pennington
All rights reserved. Published by Dr. A. Yvonne V. Pennington

ISBN-13: 978-0-6151-6532-5

First Edition, September 2007

No part of this publication may be reproduced, or stored in a retrieval system, or transmitted in any form or by any means, electronic, mechanical, photocopying, recording, or otherwise without written permission of the publisher. For permission information contact Dr. A. Yvonne V. Pennington via her website at http://www.ypsychology.com

PENNINGTON POSITIVE PARENTING

Introduction:

This workbook is written for the parents who struggle with intense children who often have a mind of their own when parents try to get them to do things. It is meant for the parents of kids who are so lethargic or laid back that nothing seems to motivate them to do the daily tasks that are required. We parents worry that we are training the next nominee for the Slacker Hall or Fame. It is geared to assist in helping kids get homework and chores done without the battles so often that come hand in hand with trying to get a person to do something he's not particularly interested in doing. By using this workbook parents can perform their own extreme family makeover.

This workbook is for parents who fly by the seat of their pants because they got nothing else to go on. It is for parents who lie awake at night worrying about what they're doing wrong. It is for parents who are afraid to answer the phone because it too often is someone from school calling because Timmy has gotten sent out of the classroom once again. It is for parents who promised themselves as kids they'd do it differently when they were grownups but find themselves falling into old habits too often.

This parenting course has been a centerpiece of my life's work. It seems that now my newest way to reach and serve others is to make this approach more available to more people. I am filled with gratitude to have had the opportunity to have developed this human approach to parenting and to continue to share it with others. With my clinical population of patients – mostly ADHD kids – I get better improvement in six weeks of parent training than seeing the patient once per week for a whole year.

For thirty-five years as a psychologist or psycho-therapist, I've been teaching parents how to successfully change almost any negative child behavior and to do it in a positive manner. After many requests from parents to put my ideas into book form, I finally put finger to keyboard to get the book done. It is dedicated to the thousands of parents and children who have consulted me over the decades and added to my knowledge of the human condition. That these patients entrusted their hopes and dreams to me for guidance is a gift beyond measure.

Each of the many thousands of parents who have attended my parenting workshops have seen that they truly can make a huge, positive difference in the lives of their children and families. Now it's time to share that good news with many more families.

This workbook is for parents who are looking for answers as to how to raise a child who has Attention Deficit Hyperactivity Disorder or Oppositional Defiant Disorder. This course can offer you a research-based alternative or adjunct to medication. Other kids also respond well to these methods.

Before the reader assumes that I'm about to trot out the white picket fence and pose in front of it with my perfect family, let me share some of the warts and bruises in my family life. We have been affected by poverty, homelessness, child abuse, spousal abuse, alcoholism, drug abuse, abandonment, debilitating, life- threatening illnesses, neglect, multiple break ins, theft and other violence, embezzlement, and paralyzing fear from death threats, stalking, and other criminal behavior.

We've also had the good fortune to love and respect each other very much, to be able to see the good in each other and most other people, to believe in ourselves to make a difference, and to believe in the worth and dignity of all and act accordingly.

Directions for the Use of This Workbook

This workbook is best used with it's companion DVD of a live *Pennington Positive Parenting* workshop. Through many years of doing this work, I've found that unless people make the commitment to do the work to change, reading this book or any other will not change things at all.

I suggest that you put some structure to your new commitment to change. Set aside a specific time each week to devote to viewing the DVD, doing the reading and designing and implementing your behavior change project. Complete the homework in writing at the end of each chapter and do the exercises I beg of you.

Treat it as though you were in a course at college. Truth to tell, this course is far more important than any college course you will ever take. See if you can set up some incentives to help you get this done. Is it possible to do this course with your spouse, neighbor, or friend? Could you use it as the base for an informal parent group? Perhaps you could set up certain rewards that you allow for yourself for successfully completing each two chapters and viewing each of the six workshop meetings. Even better, perhaps you could arrange a contract between yourself and another parent that if you do your work, your partner will reward you in some way such as taking you out for coffee. If a partner is unavailable, don't allow this as an excuse for not getting the work done. Parenting is the single most important work we all will ever do. Give your family the gift of becoming a more positive version of yourself. Give your child or children the gift of a more secure base from which to launch their lives. By letting them know daily of your unconditional love, you are well on your way to helping create more confident, cooperative, contributing children. Such people are happier and healthier to boot. You brought them into this world; they deserve your best shot at building a great launching pad.

Please don't just tell yourself, "I'll try," to get through the course. Instead make this promise to yourself and your family, just like you don't just try to get up out of your chair but you actually do it, "I'll not just try, I will do the reading, the writing, the viewing, the project. I'll just do it!"

Table of Contents

CH	CHAPTER CONTENTS	PG.
1	THE ENVIRONMENT TEACHES ALL OF US	6
2	IMPORTANT WAYS PARENTS CAN CHANGE A BEHAVIOR	24
3	A SINGLE MOTHER ACCOMPLISHES ASTOUNDING CHANGES IN HER SON	39
4	ORDINARY PARENTS TEACH NEW BEHAVIORS POSITIVELY	52
5	MORE TIPS FOR DESIGNING AND IMPLEMENTING SUCCESSFUL TOKEN ECONOMIES	84
6	NUTS AND BOLTS FOR SUCCESSFUL BEHAVIOR MODIFICATION PROJECTS	105
7	PHYSICAL, SOCIAL, AND PSYCHOLOGICAL UNDERPINNINGS OF ADHD, AND WHAT TO DO ABOUT THEM	138
8	HOW TO LISTEN SO YOUR KIDS WILL TALK	181
9	MANAGE YOUR STRESS BEFORE IT MANAGES YOU	195
10	WHAT TO DO 'TIL THE PSYCHOLOGIST COMES	222

CHAPTER 1

THE ENVIRONMENT TEACHES ALL OF US

> I HATE IT, BUT MY ENVIRONMENT SHAPES WHAT I DO, HOW I DO IT, WHAT I WEAR AND HOW I WEAR IT.

I'm vacationing at the beach with my sons, Wynn and Ty, their girlfriends and Wynn's daughter. It is a hot July day. I start to get dressed to walk down from my hotel to meet them on the beach. My skin burns easily. I'd like to wear just my bathing suit, but I have no way of getting sunscreen on my back alone, so I must cover up head-to-toe. Since I will be walking about a mile, I have to wear comfy shoes instead of the glamorous sandals from Bali I would have liked. "You can't wear that big straw beach hat you got in Miami," I tell myself. "You'll burn the back of your neck if you don't wear the Safari hat instead, the one with the neck flap that has the clip to keep it from flying away on this windy day."

I have asthma, usually under good control, but I don't dare walk that far without an emergency supply of medicine. My asthma is a result of a combination of environmental forces and inherited predisposition. Many years ago I went to the doctor and was determined to be suffering from kidney stones. A series of X-Rays with IVP dye was ordered at the local hospital. I nearly died.... my doctor and I discovered I was extremely allergic to the dye. Much of my life is now controlled by what the *environment* did to me on that fateful day.

Today, on this lovely beach day decades later, I think, " I'll need my 'Epi' pen for emergencies in case there are bees." Since I don't carry a heavy handbag due to two herniated discs in my neck from car accidents, I strap all my gear along with a bottle of water around my waist. I finally tell myself I'm ready, so I leave my air-conditioned room to brave the heat of the beach to join my sons.

Once downstairs in the lobby I notice "Fresh Paint" signs so I take a deep breath, hold it, and run through the lobby to get outside and head for the beach. Fresh paint activates my asthma and other allergies, which have left me struggling for breath many times, each lasting for hours or days. I get outside and find I'm in quite a dilemma. I have forgotten my sunglasses and a towel for the beach. Do I sprint back through the lobby to get the missing supplies or risk squinting so badly that I can barely see and sitting uncomfortably on the sand without a towel? Or maybe, I could just get in the car and drive to buy glasses and a towel and meet my family by car, but I need the exercise. Besides, I can't get to my car without going through the lobby.

I take a deep breath, hold it, and charge through the lobby, grateful the elevator door is open. I retrieve my sunglasses and a towel from my room, and once again sprint across the lobby holding my breath. I head for beach and the mile-long walk.

My environment has dictated my behavior for two hours now. Yes, some genetic predisposition added to the load, because I come from a long line of folks – five siblings and my mother - who have died of respiratory or allergy problems. My inherited light skin was sunburned badly several times when I was a child. The environment taught me then that unless I wear sunscreen and cover up well at the beach, I end up quite miserable.

After the mile-long walk on the beach I finally meet up with my family, and we proceed to have an absolute blast together. We were all having such a good time we didn't notice how long we were on the beach. Wynn and Ty didn't put on any sunscreen and got a little sunburned. The fact that we were enjoying each other contributed to our staying a longer time.

The point I'm getting to is that our environment really does shape our lives and our behavior much more than we like to think. Most of us like to think that we are in charge of our lives and our destiny, but our environment shapes us in subtle ways that are often beyond our awareness. Had I not been injected with a dye in a hospital and gone into anaphylactic shock because I was allergic to it, I would not have to run across lobbies when I see wet paint. I would not have had to give up my career as the owner of my own dance studio to find something I love that I could do sitting down, such as my chosen field of psychology.

There are many children with inherited disorders such as Attention Deficit Hyperactivity Disorder, which predispose them to be more likely to exhibit certain behaviors. Other disabilities such as specific learning disorders, autism, mental retardation, epilepsy, speech and hearing impairments, anxiety disorders, and some depression have a physical component, but the severity of the symptom presentation has much to do with the environment.

For decades there has been a lot of research documenting a genetic component to many mental and physical conditions. So for several decades more and more scientists have started to believe that genetics control most behavioral disabilities. But a newer line of research is showing that the expression of genes has much to do with the environment. For example, Dr. John Crabbe in the journal *Science* reported that in genetically identical mice, major differences occurred in mice behavior due to minor differences in their environment such as the way they were handled.

Dr. Michael Meaney has discovered that the expression of various genes in mice depends on how they are parented. Mice that are licked and groomed by their mothers become more confident, smarter, and more adventurous than baby mice not given this kind of care.

My own family has such a story. My oldest sister Agnes was born at home in an run-down shack without central heat or plumbing. She was so tiny that the attending doctor would not complete a certificate of live birth saying she would not last through the night. She wasn't weighed then either, but the story goes that her arms were the size of an adult pinky finger and a silver dollar could cover her face. My mother was the quintessential nurturer. She kept Agnes on a tiny satin pillow wrapped in blankets she had sewn herself, tucked in beside the only fireplace in the house. She held her and cuddled her most of the day when Agnes wasn't warmed by the fire. My mother slept with the baby, keeping her warm and nurtured, stroking her, singing to her, and sending love and caring to her in her voice, thoughts and prayers.

At her six weeks' checkup, the doctor was astounded to see Agnes alive, well, and thriving. She weighed in at two pounds at that check-up having gained a good bit of weight. She was a miracle baby: no incubator, no ICU, no hospital, just a loving mother's nurturing and care. Agnes grew up to be smart, confident, hard working, and outgoing. She never met a stranger. Her goodness was everywhere. Her compassion was famous in our small town.

We as parents, just like these mice parents and my mother, have an amazing opportunity to change the environment of our children to achieve remarkable results. Remember, I'm not saying that bad parenting causes Attention Deficit Hyperactivity Disorder or any other chronic condition. I'm saying that we parents can make dramatic changes in the severity of symptoms. In effect the only people we can truly change are ourselves, but in so doing we can make dramatic changes in our children's behavior.

For many decades conventional wisdom said that to change a child's behavior, he had to spend years in talk therapy until the "Ah ha!" time came when the child understood why he behaved the way he did. Then his behavior was supposed to dramatically change for the better after this insight.

It usually didn't happen. When a behavioral approach was first put forward in the psychological community, a lot of nay sayers said if you only focused on changing the behavior, it would inevitably result in symptom substitution. That is, another symptom would pop up as bad or worse than the first unless insight-oriented therapy was done. That has not happened either. For decades now psychologists have been working on changing behaviors without worrying about any deep-rooted causes, and what usually happens is that once the child's life improves by changing a behavior in one area, a snow ball effect happens and more areas of her life get better.

There are some cases in which the mental health professional must work on dealing with the root emotional cause of some children's behaviors. There is the grieving child who has suffered death or loss. Children who have suffered abuse often carry emotional scars that must be healed for a good therapeutic outcome. Depth psychotherapeutic work in these cases should be done often in addition to behavioral treatments. The depth psychotherapeutic work I do with kids, teens and adults usually has one component called Sandplay.

Sandplay is a form of of depth psychotherapy founded on the work of Dr. Carl G. Jung. It's a wonderful, creative, fun way to work through deeper issues than cannot be touched by a behavioral approach. Several years of Sandplay therapy cured my food allergies so that now I can eat anything I want. Before that depth work, I was so allergic to every food in the American diet that I had to daily choose between eating and breathing. Many patient problems presented in my office are improved by a combination of behavior modification, cognitive behavior therapy, and the depth work of Sandplay.

LEARNED VERSUS UNLEARNED BEHAVIOR

How do we as parents set about changing troublesome behaviors in our children? First we must check out our beliefs about human behaviors. We humans have a vast repertoire of behaviors. Some as simple as touching your elbow to behaviors as complex as delicate surgery in the brain or taking apart a computer, programming it, and putting it back together again. When I ask the question, "How much of this vast repertoire of human behavior is unlearned?" I get lots of different answers. Some people guess that thirty percent, even fifty percent of our behavior is unlearned.

I say the amount of unlearned behavior in our repertoire is tiny - infinitesimal. When babies are born, they can only do a few things: suck, swallow, cry, wiggle their arms and legs, eliminate waste, blink their eyes, exhibit a few reflexes such as the startle reflex, and little else. All the rest of the vast amount of behaviors are learned. How do we learn it? The environment teaches it to us. Yes, there might be an inherited pre-disposition for certain behaviors to be more likely to show up, but the environment can offer a leash that restrains the intensity and severity that the behaviors might demonstrate. This is extremely good news! What a ray of sunshine!

It means that since our behavior and that of our children are learned, therefore they can be unlearned and replaced with new, more appropriate behavior. We, as parents, can teach our children the behaviors we'd like to see them exhibit. We don't have to be stuck in simply reacting to behaviors that frustrate us. We can go about the task of being teachers of the behaviors necessary to succeed in the world. Wow, what a concept!

KIDS TEACH ADULTS, TOO

Now that we aware of the fact that we can teach behaviors, let's look at how that might work when our children actually teach us.

Dad is driving his young daughters home from a visit to Grandma's house where they have filled up on all sorts of cookies and candy. It's been an hour drive and eight-year-old twins, Sarah and Sandy, are getting restless and bored. Sarah whines, "Daddy, can we stop for ice cream?"

"Yeah, I'm hungry," chimes in Sandy.

"No, we're almost home and dinner will be waiting," replies dad as he fights the traffic.

"But, we're hot and hungry," chime in both girls. The whining and pleading continue non-stop increasing in decibel and intensity. Finally Sandy pipes up, "Daddy, why don't you just buy us the ice cream and shut us up."

What keen observation of human behavior is shown by this little girl. Of course, Dad buys the ice cream, insuring that the twins eat no dinner and that the next time they want sweets, they will whine non-stop until a parent gives in. He has taught his girls well that if they are obnoxious enough, they can get their wishes. They reward Dad for giving in to them by not bugging him any more that day. The environment, the twins, have shaped Dad's behavior by reinforcing his giving the girls what they want even if it is not healthy for them.

Here's the way it works:

ANTECEDENT ----------> BEHAVIOR ---------------> CONSEQUENCE

KIDS WHINE ------------> DAD GIVES IN ----------> KIDS ARE QUIET

STIMULUS ---------------> RESPONSE --------------> STIMULUS

We parents get into a trap in that the noxious behavior stops if we yell loud enough or give in to a child's demands. We are rewarded by the environment, thus we are that much more likely to repeat the behavior again, just to make the noise (or other unwanted behavior) stop. All of this happens below our level of awareness, unless we really start to pay attention to it.

How do your children teach you to behave differently than you'd hoped?

_____

_____

_____

_____

_____

Back when I managed my own dance studio, I remember that I would yell loud and long when class was about to start while the tap dancers were busy making as much noise as possible with their shoes. When my yelling reached a certain level of loudness and irritation, the tappers would finally get quiet. I was trained (or reinforced) to yell loud and long by the stimulus the environment gave back to me: the tappers got quiet. So next time I wanted quiet in tap class, with this kind of reinforcement of my behavior, I was much more likely to resort to the same behavior even though I didn't like doing it.

```
LOUD TAPPING -------> TEACHER YELLS -------> TAPPING STOPS
STIMULUS --------------> RESPONSE ---------------> STIMULUS
ANTECEDENT ---------> BEHAVIOR ---------------->CONSEQUENCE
```

Yes, our environment shapes our behavior in many ways - many more ways than we think. Can we stop the environment from shaping us? No, not really, but an awareness of the rules that govern behavior will serve as a powerful tool for change. By knowing how to change our environment and that of our children, we can make dramatic changes in behavior and we can do it positively.

Kids behave the way they do to avoid negative consequences or to gain access to something they deem pleasant. So do adults. We all want attention and validation, and we will get it from others in whatever ways we deem necessary. It is amazing what a child will do to wrench attention from a parent. How much positive attention do you give your child regularly?

TYPICAL PARENT COMPLAINTS

Parents have attended my *Pennington Positive Parenting* course to address these kinds of complaints:

He never listens.	He never obeys.
She whines all the time.	He takes forever to get his homework.
I'm so frustrated with this kid.	I'm yelling all the time at him.
He hangs back from any challenge.	He doesn't stop and think.
He lies about his homework and chores.	I lose my patience with him.
She won't go to bed when it's time.	She won't get up and get dressed.

WHAT BUGS YOU?

Add your complaints here:

_____

_____

_____

_____

All these can be unlearned and replaced by other behaviors.

Add your ideas about what you could change right now in your home to interact in a more positive manner:

_____

_____.

_____

_____

Lets talk about the human growth hierarchy that is the basis of movement toward more and more mental health. Movement from *self* and toward *others* is therapeutic. Movement up the levels from total self involvement and minimal awareness all the way to leadership, advocacy and mentorship is therapeutic and demonstrates growth.

Eventually, if we are very, very lucky and stay in this fine-tuned awareness, helping and teaching become second nature. New behaviors are cemented and movement toward leadership skills happens. The new behaviors are practiced long enough to become habits. Then we can become advocates and mentors for our children and other families. It all starts with awareness - being able to look honestly at what is happening.

HUMAN GROWTH HIERARCHY

(start at bottom & work up)

OTHERS   **OTHERS**

MENTORSHIP

ADVOCACY

LEADERSHIP

POSITIVE REGARD

HELPING AND TEACHING

INTEGRATED ACTION

PLANNING

DIRECTION

INDEPENDENCE

INTERACTION

UNDERSTANDING

RESPONSIBILITY

ACCEPTANCE

RECOGNITION

AWARENESS

Δ   **SELF**   Δ

Notice that movement goes from total self involvement at the bottom of the page up and out toward others. Before we can do any teaching of new behaviors, we must step back, observe, and become more aware of what is going on in the first place. Just that act of stepping back and becoming more objective is huge. Developing awareness is a necessary first step to changing anything. We need to develop an awareness of how little we listen to our children and how little we pay attention to them when they're behaving well. In developing an awareness, we start to recognize patterns just as a scientist observes patterns. We can even pretend this child is someone else's and figure out what we might suggest to this other fantasy parent. After a while of doing such observation, active reflection and objectivity, we can start to accept our part in creating some of the problem. Next we can start to accept some responsibility as we develop more understanding of the dynamics in the family. Then we will probably start to do more interaction rather than mere reaction. Our behavior becomes independent as we become more systematic and focused. We achieve more goal direction in our parenting. With planning we arrive at more integrated action. Our roles shift from disciplinarian to that of helping and teaching. We actually develop more positive regard for our kids and ourselves. Our parenting style develops more of the positive qualities of good leadership such as encouragement, a sense of humor, and better listening.

More qualities of good leadership we can develop in ourselves and our children include openness to new experiences, risk tolerance, self-regulation skills, and goal orientation. These qualities of good leadership become part of who we are and who our children are becoming. We start to keep in mind more and more that our ultimate goal is building confident, competent, contributing, caring adults. We learn to motivate rather than discourage. We learn to collaborate with our families toward a common good.

Other qualities associated with good leadership include intelligence, extroversion, and consideration of others, to name a few. Also good leaders are able to establish mutual trust, two-way communication, rapport, and concern for the other regardless of the work produced. Lowin and Craig in 1968 found the markings of good leadership in one's ability to remain considerate and supportive in spite of the ineffectiveness of the people being led. Tall order for us, but ideals to aspire to in our journey to change our world one family at a time.

REVIEW AND HOMEWORK FOR CHAPTER 1

1. A huge majority of human behaviors is _____.

2. Behaviors are learned from interaction with the _____.

3. Even though many conditions are at least in part genetic and probably inherited, parents can help reduce the symptom presentation by changing the _____.

4. When behavior problems are treated by changing the behavior rather than doing depth psychotherapy for years to get to the root cause, _____ symptom substitution usually occurs.

5. The first step in changing any behavior is _____.

6. For the next week choose one meal time when the whole family is together and count the number of positive comments you make to members of your family during that 20-30 minutes of meal time. Write down the count here:_____.

7. For three whole minutes listen, really listen to your child. Don't try to plan what you will say or solve the problem for her. Just listen.

8. Human behavior is generally considered to be influenced by heredity along with _____.

9. Since we cannot change our genetic makeup, we can make changes in our own or others' behavior by changing the _____.

10. The majority of human behaviors are _____(learned or unlearned).

11. When something happens in the environment that is pleasant, the behavior that happens right before the happening is _____.

12. When a behavior is reinforced, another word for this is _____.

13. List three behaviors in your child you'd like to see increased:

    _____

    _____.

14. List three behaviors in your child you'd like to see decreased:

    _____

    _____.

answers: I. learned II. environment III. environment IV. no V. awareness VI, VII: (varies) VIII. environment IX. environment X. learned XI. reinforced, XII. rewarded

CHAPTER ONE

MY PLAN FOR IMPROVEMENT

My plan for improvement in my awareness and objectivity is

_____

I will know my plan is effective when_____

I plan to do these less (circle all that apply): nag, criticize, give in to whining, interrupt, warning without follow through, etc. _____.

I plan to do these more (circle all that apply) listen, act more firmly, be kinder, notice good behavior, improve my patience, etc,_____

My specific goals for the next week are:

Monday:_____

Tuesday_____

Wednesday_____

Thursday_____

Friday_____

Saturday_____

Sunday_____

Complete this page, photocopy it, carry it with you daily.

Download all the Improvement Plans and other fillable sheets in this workbook in a companion printable file:

http://www.ypsychology.com/downloads/ppp/ipworkbook.zip

Password: ***PPPIPWorkbook*** *(case sensitive)*

CHAPTER 2

IMPORTANT WAYS PARENTS CAN CHANGE BEHAVIORS

Since almost all behavior is learned, it is taught by the environment. The environment includes our family as well as the people we encounter at school and in the community. All these folks end up being our teachers because the environment teaches us new behaviors.

Attention from other people is a basic human desire and need. Withdraw that attention and we will do almost anything to get it back. Sometimes it doesn't matter whether it is negative or positive attention as long as people pay attention to us.

Take Jamie (not his real name) for example. He was five when I met him and driving his parents crazy because he refused to go to bed at night. When he was first born, he had had respiratory problems so his parents got used to a regimen of checking in on him a lot around bedtime. By the time I saw him, he hadn't had any respiratory problems for four years. But when eight o'clock rolled around, his campaign to stay awake longer started with a vengeance. He needed another trip to the bathroom, another bedtime story, another cup of hot chocolate. Could he please just stay up a little longer to watch the next television program? He had just one more burning question to ask mom or dad. And on and on it went. The parents had no couple-ship time at the end of the day. Their marriage was going downhill. They bickered constantly over the best way to deal with Jamie. Little did they know that they were inadvertently rewarding the very behavior they wanted so desperately to eliminate. No parent sets out to deliberately make a brat of a child, but we do it nevertheless by remaining unaware of the laws governing human behavior.

My first task was to help the parents develop a better awareness of what exactly was going on. Their first assignment was to step back and look at the problem objectively. I asked them when his bedtime was. It was 8 P.M. I asked when he finally fell asleep. Ten o'clock was the answer. This persistent youngster would finally fall asleep after two hours of the parents exhausting themselves exhorting with, "Shut up and go to sleep!" Their yelling and screaming at him got more intense each night as the hour got later.

My recommendations were these: Tonight Mr. And Mrs. Andrews (not their real name) were to make sure they gave Jamie lots of hugs and kisses and reassured him of their love and support frequently, but particularly at bed time. They were to help him beforehand with a plan if he felt bored, wide awake, lonely or scared. He could look at a book if he was bored, count his slow deep breaths to help him get sleepy, and hug a stuffed animal and look at his parents' pictures if he felt lonely. He could hide in his cozy bed tent that parents had sprayed with "monster repellent" right before bedtime and remember that all the doors and windows were locked and the closet was free of monsters if he felt scared. BUT, then they were to put Jamie to bed. Their instructions were to him that since he was supposed to be asleep after eight P.M, they would pretend he was asleep after that until morning. If he got out of bed, he would be put back in bed immediately without anyone looking at him or talking to him. If he called out to them, they would not answer.

What is your guess as to whether the behavior got worse or better at first? You probably guessed that it got worse. Bingo! It got much worse. Such a program is called an extinquishment regimen. We know a lot about how people behave when reinforcement is withdrawn from a behavior that was previously reinforced. Jamie had been reinforced for his negative bedtime behavior for years. He got attention even if it was negative attention. When we yell at our kids, we are giving them our attention. We all crave attention. If we can't get positive attention - you guessed it – we will try to get negative attention. Nature abhors a vacuum and so does the human psyche. We want to be noticed. Often we parents pay attention – negative attention - to the wrong behaviors, and we unwittingly ensure that the behaviors we don't like will continue unabated.

Psychologists have a term for the worsening of behavior when reinforcement is withdrawn. This phenomenon is called the <u>extinction burst</u> and it usually lasts about three days. Indeed for Jamie, and particularly his parents, those three days were horrible. I told the parents to call the neighbors and assure them they weren't committing child abuse; they were just insisting their five year old go to bed on time. The Andrews stuck to their guns. They didn't give in and talk to him or let him watch just one more program on television. After three days we had a cure. Jamie went to bed at eight without a peep after the usual story, hug, reassurance and praise for being such a grown-up boy. He got his good-night kiss and was fast asleep within minutes.

The parents were able to reconnect as a couple. They could actually sit down in the evening and have a conversation and catch up on each other's individual lives. What a wonderful thing to be able to be in charge of your household again instead of its being run by a five year old. This example does not mean that I encourage parents not to come to the aid of a child who is frightened, sick, sad or lonely sometimes at bedtime. This example is about how certain behaviors can become bad habits and need a systematic program to help them change.

The cure for Jamie lasted for several months until Grandma paid a visit for a week. During that time she assured the parents they had no idea how to raise this poor, pitiful child who was crying his sad, little eyes out each night for Grandma to rock him, give him another chocolate chip cookie, and to read him just one more bedtime story. The whole time Grandma was there Jamie just lapped up all that attention he got for backsliding into his past onerous behavior. He was wide awake until at least ten o'clock every night.

Eventually Grandma left and things went back to normal, right? Wrong! There was another extinction burst. This time it lasted only two days. The Andrews stuck with the program and ignored his pleading and whining, knowing he was not thirsty, hungry, scared or lonely. He wouldn't die if he didn't get just one more hug from dad before he fell asleep, particularly since Mom and Dad had made sure lots of affection and positive attention were his before bedtime. So we finally did really get a permanent cure.

Believe me, I've seen fifteen-year-old kids still sleeping with their parents, because the parents just weren't up to insisting that the child grow up a bit and sleep alone. That's not love, it's indifference to the child's true need for independence. The parents made the mistake of just feeling too sorry for the youngster who cried so long and hard when expected to sleep independently. Remember there's nothing wrong with comforting a child who's had a nightmare once in a while, or seeing after a child who is having an an unusually hard time getting to sleep on a rare occasion. This plan is for the child who habitually is up late, refusing to engage in any behavior that might induce sleep.

Paying attention to the laws that govern behavior, we note that ignoring a behavior can result in making it go away. Remove the reinforcement from a behavior and you will see it eventually die out. One of the best ways to get rid of temper tantrums is to walk out of the room. The child will eventually tire of all that energy being expended if there is no audience.

I do not recommend that a policy of ignoring a behavior be used to eliminate or weaken dangerous behaviors. Imagine ignoring a child playing in the street and hoping she doesn't get killed before she gets the notion that playing in the street is not a good idea.

Also, as shown in Grandma's visit to the Andrews home, everyone has to be on board for ignoring to work in teaching a new behavior. If a school bus driver tries to ignore one child's unruly behavior while all the other kids pay attention to it, the plan will not work. If Mom decides to ignore a child's behavior, but Dad can't stand it anymore and yells at the youngster, the ignoring will not work.

There's another way to teach new behaviors. Punish the bad behavior. This is not news to any reader. Parents have been using punishment for generation after generation. If punishment were all that effective, bad behavior would probably have been eliminated by now. But bad behavior has persisted because even though punishment is often necessary, it does have some problems. One of the problems, particularly if physical punishment is used, is that the child is now spending a huge amount of emotional energy thinking about how mad he is at the parent, rather than thinking about how he can change. If the whole idea is to help the child learn different ways to behave, programs that have the child spending lots of energy thinking about how mad he is at Mom or Dad are not going to be nearly as effective as programs in which the child is spending energy figuring out how to please the parents and get more positive attention.

Another problem with punishment is that it typically requires lots of repetition in different environments before the behavior is learned and changed. It has been my experience that teaching by punishment means that the learning doesn't generalize as well as learning created by other methods. Also, physical punishment really interferes dramatically with the parent-child relationship. It hinders the development of the safe haven of security that we all need to be able to tackle the world with confidence and self reliance. Discipline should not be about making the child feel bad or hurting the child. Some misguided souls even advocate "breaking the child's will." A person without some self will and self determination will not make good decisions as an adult. Effective punishment has the purpose of teaching and guiding. It is training to help the child achieve socially desirable behavior toward becoming a good citizen.

To be effective, physical punishment must be escalated often. A slap on the rear may work initially, but later you may have to escalate to a belt to teach the same lesson. Also, if you're trying to teach a youngster not to hit by hitting him, the child doesn't understand the poor logic. Also it's been my experience that most physical punishment is done in anger when we parents are out of control. That is not discipline; it is revenge.

So for just this short while during the course of reading this book, keep doing what you've always done before except I'd like to encourage you to forgo physical punishment. The rule of the house should be: "PEOPLE ARE NOT FOR HITTING."

Easier ways to remember this are rhymes I tell parents:

 WANNA WHACK? TURN YOUR BACK.
WANNA FUME? LEAVE THE ROOM.
WANNA SEETHE? JUST BREATHE.

Letting go of old habits is hard, but we do need to stop venting our anger on our kids. This doesn't mean we will never punish. Not on your life. Later in this workbook we will tackle effective punishment. There are some kids who require punishment for them to be able to change. I encourage Time Out for many children, and I will go into more detail about how to do this properly and effectively at a later point in this workbook.

For now I implore you as a parent to exercise self control. Did I always do this? No. Any parent who says she has never lost her temper with her children is either lying or a saint, and I haven't heard of any canonizations lately. I know I ain't no saint!

It is important to know that research published by Drs. Park and Peterson in the <u>Journal of Adolescence</u> shows that parents who exercise self control have happier children. That does make sense. If a child can count on stability of mood and behavior from his parent, that child is free to explore the world with curiosity and self confidence - some of the most important stepping stones to adult happiness. These are important building blocks for the eventual competent, confident adult you want your child to be.

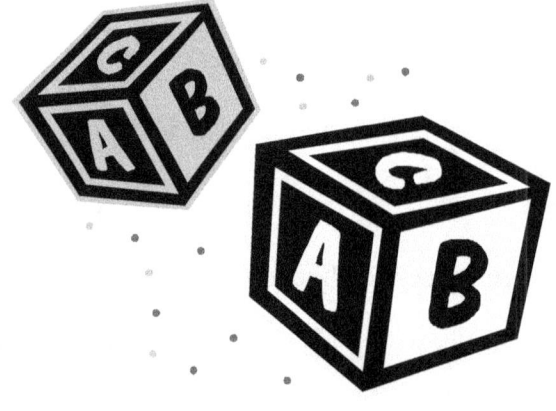

For now we will focus on positive methods to achieve change in our children's behavior. The single most effective way to teach a new behavior is to find a behavior that is incompatible – usually the opposite – to the behavior you want to change. For example, if a teacher wants to get her class to stop running around the room and stop yelling, what should she do? You might suggest that she scream, "Quiet!" loudly, repeatedly and turn the light switch on and off rapidly. That could work, but a better way would be to praise the first youngster who is seated and quiet. An even better ides would be to set up a system by which the first child seated and quiet for five minutes earns the privilege of being lunch line leader that day. Later ten then twenty minutes, and on up would be required to earn the reward.

Dr. Ken Matheny at Georgia State University way back in 1973 found that teachers give out a ratio of twelve to one negative to positive comments to students daily. After 26 weeks of intensive training and support, these same teachers were able to claim two-year achievement gains in their students as well as true and lasting gains in self esteem for their charges. The training the teachers got was much like the training in this course: how to focus on positives versus negatives. By the end of the study, these wonderful teachers learned to change their comments to their students to a ratio of one negative to thirteen positive.

So we know from research that without intervention most teachers tend to be more negative than positive. The same goes for parents, too. Adults tend to scold, mock, deprive, and even strike kids more than they offer kindness and encouragement. It's been my experience that most of us parents if we are really honest, admit that we focus on the bad behavior more than the good. Most parents will focus on the F's and D's on the report card rather than the A's and B's, even when they are equal in number. During this course we are going to change that.

Here's a cardinal rule of behavior. Whatever comes right after the target behavior controls whether or not that behavior will be repeated or will drop out of the behavioral repertoire of things the person does often in that particular environment. It's that same:

Stimulus -----> Response -----> Stimulus

It's the second stimulus - something that happens in the environment immediately and consistently after a behavior - that teaches a new behavior. Two very important words: *Immediately and Consistently*. The second stimulus determines whether or not the behavior will be repeated or eventually drop out of the behavioral repertoire.

Psychologists first learned this law of behavior by working with animals. They found that if they consistently and immediately rewarded pigeons, mice, dogs, chimps, and all kinds of animals, they were able to teach them to do incredible stunts never thought possible before. It is a law of behavior just like Newton's law of physics. If an apple is dropped from a tree, it will fall. If you reinforce appropriate, pro-social behaviors consistently and immediately for a short while, your child's behavior <u>will</u> change for the better.

Sometimes you can change behavior by changing the first stimulus, the event in the environment that occurs before the behavior in question. For example, if every time Jimmy and Johnny sit near each other in class, they get disruptive, a good idea would be to remove the initial stimulus of the two sitting together. The problem is, we can't always do something about events that precede behaviors we are concerned about. We can't always keep siblings apart. We, as parents, can't design seating charts for schools. At home, though, we can carefully look as what happens after our child does something we don't like and start to see patterns in the family interactions. We can get more perspective on what we could do differently rather than focusing totally on how we can punish the child to make him stop.

Paying attention to the event that happens right after a behavior we like will be the major thrust of the behavior change systems discussed in this book. These events that follow a behavior reinforce a behavior if the event is a pleasurable one. Of course, if a desired behavior is reinforced, this means that the encouraged behavior is more like to recur.

Another way to look at this is with the rule that worked well in my family: first you work, then you play. It's almost impossible to get Charlie back inside to do his homework if he's allowed to play outside first. If the scenario is reversed, Charlie earns an activity reinforcer – playing outside – by completing his homework correctly and promptly.

The positive attention we will use after a behavior we'd like to nurture is called a social reinforcer or praise. In general we think of praise as a good thing, but under certain circumstances it can actually do the opposite of what we want it to achieve for us. In

2007 in the <u>Journal of Child Development</u> Dr. Carol Dweck reported on a very interesting study. She and her colleagues at Columbia University in New York have spent more than ten years studying the affects of different types of praise on children. She studied several hundred fourth and fifth graders in public schools, randomly assigning them to two groups. The children were given the same I.Q. test using puzzles. The puzzles were easy enough so that all the subjects did well. When the test results were shared with the kids, one group was told, "You must be smart at this." The other group who had done equally as well were told, "You must have worked really hard."

Next all the kids were given a choice: to take another harder test that would teach them more about problem solving or to take another test just like the first. Ninety percent of the children praised for their hard work opted for a new challenge. The kids who had been told they were smart hedged, choosing the easy road. These kids seemed worried about risking being "not so smart" next time and were unwilling to put their egos on the line.

The next step in the study involved giving all the kids a test that was very hard, designed for children two years older than they. Everyone failed. The kids that had been praised for their effort realized they needed to get involved, trying different solutions. Many of this group said the harder test was their favorite one. The kids praised for being smart assumed their failure meant they were not really smart after all.

In a later test as easy as the first the kids praised for effort improved their original scores by 30%. The children praised for being smart did worse on this test by 20%. It seems that since effort is something kids can control, the kids who were praised for the process of problem solving and their hard work, increased their effort with good results.

The kids who were told they had a naturally high intelligence, were robbed of any good way to respond to the inevitable failure we all encounter sometime.

There were several conclusions Dr. Dweck took from her study. We need to praise the process. Specific praise rather than global, generic praise works best. Credibility and sincerity seem important as well. Also she has found that if there is praise and then it stops, the effort withers away. She suggests, as many other researchers have, that we switch to intermittent reinforcement to keep a behavior going. She also suggests letting kids know that the brain is like a muscle and that working it – just like exercise improves other muscles – makes it grow new connections.

REVIEW AND HOMEWORK FOR CHAPTER 2

1. If parents systematically ignore a difficult behavior consistently, will the behavior immediately get better? Yes ___ No _____

2. When reinforcement is removed from a behavior, and the child tries harder to get the parents to revert back to their previous behavior, this worsening of symptoms is called an _____.

3. Is ignoring recommended for dangerous behaviors? Yes___ No____

4. Is physical punishment recommended? Yes____ No___

5. A very good way to change behavior in a youngster is to systematically _____ the desired behavior.

6. The best two ways to change behaviors is to use positive reinforcement _____ and _____.

7. One type of reinforcer that is very useful is an _____ reinforcer.

8. In the natural environment teachers (and probably parents, too) have a ratio of __ negative to __ positive comments.

9. With training and support teachers were able to have a ratio of ___ negative to ___ positive comments.

10. To work well and not decrease kids' work output, praise the _____, _____, and _____.

11. To be helpful praise should be _____, _____, and _____.

12. The key to teaching perseverance is eventually ___ rewarding every achievement.

13. _____ reinforcement keeps the effort coming after the behavior is learned.

14. Keep track of the frequency and intensity of one target behavior you child does. Find out how long he can go without doing it.

answers: I. no II. extinction burst III. no IV. no V. reinforce or reward VI. consistently and immediately VII. activity, social VIII. one, twenty-one IX. one, thirteen X. effort, process, concentration XI. sincere, truthful, specific. XII. not XIII. intermittent

CHAPTER TWO

MY PLAN FOR IMPROVEMENT

My plan for improvement in recognizing the patterns of behavior in my family and accepting my part in them

is_____

_____

The way I'll know my plan is working

is_____

I plan to do these *less* (circle all that apply): scold, strike, shame, harass, yell, threaten, etc_____.

I plan to do *more* of these (circle all that apply): listen, encourage, communicate, support, make time for family fun, notice good behavior, praise effort and hard work, etc_____.

My specific plan for change is:

Monday_____

Tuesday_____

Wednesday_____

Thursday_____

Friday_____

Saturday_____

Sunday_____

Complete this page, photocopy it, and carry it with you daily.

CHAPTER 3

A SINGLE MOTER ACCOMPLISHES ASTOUNDING CHANGES IN HER SON'S ANGER MANAGEMENT

A five-year-old boy called Jerry (not his real name) displayed severe temper tantrums almost daily - often several times a day. If he was asked to pick up his toys, a tirade started. If he was told to brush his teeth, he fell to the floor in a fit. If he made a mistake, he threw a fit. He was so irritable the slightest issue made him fall apart. He dissolved into tears and screams if his hair wasn't exactly how he wanted it.

Jerry's mother, Hazel, was assisted in designing a behavior change project. She started to realize that his tantrums had a big payoff in her paying attention to them, even if the attention was pleading with him to stop, yelling back at him, or sometimes even hitting him. Remember, we are not interested in stopping Jerry from feeling angry. Anger is a normal human emotion. We just want him to stop throwing tantrums.

I noted that Hazel rarely paid attention to Jerry when he was behaving himself. She was convinced that he was bad all the time, so there was no good behavior for which to give him attention. I asked her to time the length of the tantrums, the time between tantrums, and to keep count of how frequently he threw a tantrum.

She was also asked to rate the intensity of the tantrum on a scale from 1-5. She returned with the information that he threw a severe Level 5 tantrum about every half hour. The tantrums lasted about five minutes each, but they were known sometimes to last a half hour.

Armed with this information we were able to help Hazel design an effective behavior change plan. She was to notice Jerry and praise him every half hour or so that he did not tantrum. She was to set a timer to remind herself to go find Jerry every half hour and reinforce this wonderful absence of tantrums. She also was to reward any event or behavior in which Jerry behaved in the opposite manner than he typically had. If he handled a frustration well, Hazel was to go over to him, pat him on the back, and say how proud she was of him for handling his mad feelings like a big boy. She also was to give him a token. She chose blue poker chips, because blue was his favorite color.

Notice that she was to use several types of reinforcers. First she was using social reinforcement: praise, a wink, a high five, a hug, a thumbs up – each of these gestures are a social way to convey praise, kindness, and loving attention to someone. Praise, "Great Kid"certificates, the phrase, "'Atta' boy", and other such remarks are social reinforcers that we all crave.

She was also to give Jerry tokens very frequently. Tokens have no intrinsic value in and of themselves. They merely stand for something and allow parents to reinforce much more often than they might be able to otherwise. In this case they stand for the fun things Jerry would get to do if he had enough tokens. They reminded Jerry very frequently that refraining from his histrionics made nice things happen. For the first time in his life Jerry was assured that he would get positive attention and get to do fun things if he behaved appropriately and dealt with the frustrations of his young life in socially desirable ways. What a good lesson to learn at a very young age: you are in charge of your own destiny!

Activity reinforcers are the third type of reinforcer. These are the fun things kids love to do. These can include a board game with Mom, a card game with Dad, time on the computer, time with a video game, having a friend over, playing catch with dad, a trip to the park, calling grandma on the phone, taking photos and printing them on the computer, or using a special craft box.

Some kids get turned on by getting to choose desert for the family. This type of reinforcer is a primary or unlearned reinforcer. I keep a bucket of bubble gum in my office that I give my child patients at the end of each session if they have worked with me, stayed tuned in, and answered my questions. No one has to teach a kid to like bubble gum. I like it, too. And I love to blow bubbles, particularly in my car when I'm stuck in traffic, but the bubble blowing would be an activity reinforcer. Primary reinforcers are things we like to eat or drink. They are often sweet because it is rare that you have to teach a kid to like cake, ice cream, candy, or cookies. My favorite flavor of ice cream is butter pecan. Nobody taught me to like it. I just do.

In this course, we'll be using mostly three kinds of reinforcers as we design a behavior change project. These are activity, social, or token reinforcers. Tokens have no intrinsic value in and of themselves, but stand for the eventual reward that is coming. They can be poker chips, cut out pieces of paper, points on a chart, a stamp on the hand, or stars on a chart. Money is even a token, although we tend to give it intrinsic value for what it can buy, it really is just pieces of green paper. By the way I do not encourage use of money for rewards for kids. You may have to resort to the use of money with teens, but there are too many activity reinforcers that turn little kids on instead of money.

For most situations I don't encourage much use of primary reinforcers as part of a formal reinforcement system. But an occasional, "Harry, you've been working on your homework hard for thirty minutes. Take a break and have a snack." can be very useful sometime.

After a week of keeping track of Jerry's tantrums and their frequency, Hazel was ready to change things in a positive manner. On the first day, since she was now aware of his frequency, she worked hard at getting to Jerry with a token and praise before he had a tantrum. Jerry loved getting them and collecting them. He'd stack them up in towers and topple them over repeatedly. But what he really liked was what he was able to exchange his tokens for every two to three hours. He got to choose from a whole reinforcer menu he and Hazel had designed. She'd used pictures and drawings of the rewards he could earn and the number of chips it took to get to do these activities. Hazel drew circles the size of the chips on a colorful chart to display the cost in tokens of each activity. Jerry could line his chips up in the circles until he filled a row. It was then he knew he had enough to get to do an activity he liked. He loved being in charge now of when he could expect to get to do something fun.

While he was playing near her in the kitchen, she modeled dealing with mishaps well. She "accidentally" spilled some water on the floor and said, "Oh, I spilled some water. I had an accident. No problem. I'll be more careful next time. I'll just get a paper towel and clean that up. Oh, look, Jerry, you're handling your mistakes just like a grown up, too. Here's a token. I'm so proud of you for working hard on your writing and drawing. You made a mistake on the 'J' in your name, but you just erased it and went on. Wow, what a good way to handle mistakes. Here's another token. You're working so well and quietly at the table that it allows me to cook us a delicious lunch. And remember, you get to choose desert after lunch with all those tokens you're earning."

The first day on this new system, his tantrums diminished from his usual twelve a day to only three. An additional plus was the fact that tantrum severity declined to a score of two. His favorite activity was making cookies. That evening he turned his tokens in to help mom make his favorite: oatmeal with raisins. They even put some pecans in them. Yum! Hazel and Jerry had a party with milk and cookies to celebrate the wonderful change he was making in his handling life's irritations.

The next day he only had two very mild tantrums at the lowest level of severity, nothing like the ones he had habitually thrown. No longer was he dropping to the floor, flailing about, kicking and screaming at the top of his lungs.

Hazel was diligent about leaving the room when he threw his few fits now. She busied herself elsewhere until the minute or two of the tantrum was over. No longer was she threatening him with a spanking, loss of privileges, hitting him, yelling at him, or calling him a brat. By the fourth day, Jerry's tantrums had disappeared. Yes, he had established new habits. We now know from brain research, new neural pathways are made with changes in behavior. Now Jerry no longer seemed hard-wired to be the road-rage junkie headed for jail that he could have become.

This was an enormous change for Hazel, too. You see, she was a single parent. She got no child support; they hadn't heard from Jerry's dad for years. She worked long hours on her feet. It was only on weekends that she had any kind of time to spend with her son training him in these new ways to be. Her level of frustration and fatigue was very high. But she was soon convinced by a little training and support that she could make a difference. Her son wasn't destined to continue the bratty behavior that had become such a habit. With a little support and knowledge, this young woman turned herself into a nurturing, loving mother and her child into a happy, cooperative youngster. Her token economy gave her the framework and the reminders to immediately and consistently give her son the loving gestures, words, and positive attention he craved.

I encouraged Hazel to start with one behavior at a time so she and Jerry could be successful. Later she added more behaviors she wanted Jerry to change after he found success in eliminating tantrums.

Hazel found that by giving her son regular positive strokes that were direct, immediate and appropriate to the situation she was able to help her son feel good about himself and more enlivened in his play and interaction with her. He felt so much more important now that he got the attention he craved, but he got it now with positive behaviors. Goodwill grew amazingly fast between Hazel and Jerry during this time. She was still tired from long hours, he still missed her when she was not there, but both were no longer frustrated with each other. The positive strokes Hazel was giving Jerry were expressions of affection that were long overdue. We know that people who receive enough positive strokes themselves are able to give some back to others. Imagine what a different world it would be if each of us got several hugs and affirmations that we are appreciated each day. A one-person-at-a-time map to world peace.

WRITE SOME POSITIVE SROKES THAT YOU CAN GIVE:

_____

_____

_____

This same story has been repeated over and over in my practice with thousands of patients for more than three decades. Early in my career, I gave this *Pennington Positive Parenting* course free to the parents in the school system that employed me as their school psychologist. I had to work hard to convince the school board and the superintendent that training parents was a good thing for a school system to do. Before he would be okay with my donating my time to do it, the assistant superintendent attended one of my courses. Once he was sold, he began recommending it throughout the school system. I was not paid over-time or any pay for staying extra hours late at night to do the training when my official school work day was over at 4:00 P.M, but I believed enough in changing one family at a time. Seeing the changes in those kids was reward enough. It was amazing how soon the children in these families whose parents attended my course came to school so much happier, more attentive, and more cooperative than they had ever been before.

Once I started teaching these methods to teachers, dramatic changes in whole classes and whole schools started to happen. The referrals for my psychological services and for kids to be moved into special education dropped by half.

Some positive strokes from parents and teachers can mean so much to a child. Noticing the child, looking into her eyes down at her height level and attentively listening – really listening - to what that youngster has to say is a gift we need to bestow on our children daily. Just this much can be an enormous positive stroke – a stroke like we give so freely to a pet cat to have him purring contentedly in our laps. Could it be that bratty kids are just hungry for the missing positive strokes we parents and teachers neglect to give them? They will provoke negative attention if we starve them of our positive attention. I believe that every angry outburst is a cry for someone to notice who we are with our own needs. Such goes for kids and grown ups, spouses, friends, and co-workers. Awareness. Listening. Mindfulness. Powerful tools for change.

We hold up a mirror to our children every day through our words, actions, facial expressions, and body language. This looking glass tells the child who he is and what he came from. We can paint the picture of our child with dark, distasteful images of shame, embarrassment, sadness, and worry. We possess the power to erase such painful pictures and replace them with the bright, beautiful, glorious colors of a good self image when we praise hard work, concentration and perseverance. A child learns what he lives.

Close your eyes and take a few deep, cleansing breaths so that you get to a place of relaxation. Return in your mind way, way back into your childhood, to your earliest childhood memory. Notice the facial expression, the body language, the tone of voice and what is being said by the other people with you that day. This memory has colored your view of yourself and the world ever since. The people in your early memory held up a looking glass for you to see yourself and the world. In the same manner, you are holding up a mirror to your child, you are laying down memory tracks for you child to mold her view of the world.

We can choose to show our children the true colors they were born with. We can paint that portrait of kindness, cooperation, confidence, caring, helpfulness, patience, and love. It takes one step at a time when we notice specific instances of each. These are sign posts along the way. Reminders, mirrors back onto the self that effort and focus lead to ultimate achievement of the qualities we so much want to nurture in our children.

Here are some of the behaviors that have been successfully tackled with

Pennington Positive Parenting methods:

homework completion	classwork completion
getting ready for school on time	getting ready and in bed on time
improved hygiene	reducing temper tantrums
sibling rivalry	appropriate table manners
respectful attitudes	obeying curfew
home chores	reducing profanity
compliance with parental requests	good in-store behavior
quiet car behavior	improved social skills
sleeping alone	cooperation with siblings
bed wetting	soiling pants
reduced truancy and tardiness	reduced defiance
improved self esteem	improved anxiety/fear response
reduced depression	improved self control
reduced aggression	giving compliments
accepting "No"	reduced impulsivity
making good decisions	improved listening
improved truth telling	eliminating stealing
family cooperation	asking permission
neighborhood citizenship	reduced defiance
improved grades	improved car behavior
improved respect for authority	reduced tattling
concentration	accepting responsibility for mistakes

Time and energy devoted to noticing the appropriate behavior are the critical ingredients. It's just like watering a plant. If you water it, it will grow. If you reinforce the good behavior, it will strengthen and grow.

These behaviors listed above were changed not by telling kids how smart and great they were, which can sometimes be a big mistake. Then they might be afraid to risk or work hard, afraid they might prove you wrong.

These kids changed because the parents were using activity reinforcement, tokens and praise that was SHIC. Initially to teach a new behavior, they used praise that was:

SPECIFIC

HONEST

IMMEDIATE

CONSISTENT

Later the praise and other reinforcement was continued intermittently to keep the persistence alive and well.

REVIEW AND HOMEWORK FOR CHAPTER 3

1. The four types of reinforcers are:

    1_____ 2_____ 3_____ 4_____.

2. Another name for a reinforcer is a _____.

3. A "thumbs up" gesture would be called a _____ reinforcer.

4. Praise works best when it is S_____, H_____,

    I_____ and C_____.

5. Write some examples of activity reinforcers in this space:

    _____

    _____

    _____

6. An absence of a behavior can be strengthened by giving a _____ for a certain amount of time the child refrains from the target behavior.

7. A behavior change project should start with _____ or two behaviors at a time.

8. Write down two behaviors that your child does. After watching for a while, write down what happens right after each behavior. See if you can see a pattern and predict whether the behavior will be repeated or not. (Hint: if it is reinforced by any attention, it will be repeated.)

9. Design a behavior change project to either strengthen or weaken a chosen behavior in your child.

    What behavior will you change? _____

    Is it observable and can it be counted? _____

(9. Continued)

What types of tokens will you give and how frequently will you give them?

_____. Is the frequency of earning tokens based on baseline information as to how often the behavior happens now?

_____ What type of back up reinforcers are you offering and are they on a reinforcer menu so that small steps of improvement in behavior can be rewarded? _____

_____

Are there daily and weekly activity reinforcers to be earned?_____

Is there an opportunity for many tokens to be earned?_____.

Is there a way to keep track of the tokens earned? _____

How will you make sure the tokens are given immediately and consistently?

_____

_____.

Does the child understand what she has to do to earn tokens and other rewards?

_____

_____.

answers:

I. activity, token, social, and primary or unlearned. II. reward III. social IV. specific, honest, immediate, consistent V. games, tv, computer, reading together, petting the cat, bubble bath, etc. VI. reinforcer VII. one

50

CHAPTER THREE

MY PLAN FOR IMPROVEMENT

My plan to increase my responsibility for managing my child's behavior and my reactions to it is_____

I will know my plan is working when_____

I plan to do less of these (circle all that apply): nag, slap, scream, punish, see only the bad behavior, etc._____

I plan to do more of these (circle all that apply): listen, act with kindness, responsibility and consideration, act rather than react, become more consistent, notice good behavior immediately, give praise that is Specific, Honest, Immediate, Consistent, etc._____

The specific parts of my plan are:

Monday_____

Tuesday_____

Wednesday_____

Thursday _____

Friday_____

Saturday_____

Sunday_____

Complete this page, photocopy it, and carry it with you daily.

CHAPTER 4
ORDINARY PARENTS TEACH NEW BEHAVIORS POSITIVELY

| **Karen Learns To Get To School On Time** |

Seven-year-old Karen had a hard time getting up in the morning, getting dressed, groomed, and off to school, She dawdled while her mother repeatedly returned to her bedroom to find Karen making little progress in getting dressed. Fifteen minutes after being dragged out of bed, Karen would only manage to get her panties on. Mrs. Green nagged, complained, threatened, cajoled, screamed, and lost her temper in frustration every morning. Usually Karen waited until her mother finally dressed her is exasperation and drove her to school because she often missed the bus. Ms. Blake felt hopeless and helpless to change things on her own. When she consulted me, she was feeling like a total failure as a mother. She was sick and tired of screaming.

First I asked her mother to track for a week the percentage of her grooming and dressing tasks Karen was able to complete in the thirty minutes she was allotted each morning. Just stepping back and carefully observing what is going on develops an awareness of the specifics of the behavior, its antecedents and it's consequences, and is the beginning of designing a successful behavior change project. Karen's mother created the following list of Karen's morning tasks:

(1) get out of bed with first alarm from clock

(2) go to bathroom

(3) wash face

(4) brush teeth

(5) take off pajama top

(6) remove pajama bottom

(7) put on panties

(8) undershirt

(9) one sock

(10) second sock

(11) pants

(12) shirt

(13) one shoe

(14) the other shoe

(15) tie one shoe

(16) tie the other shoe

(17) brush hair

(18) come to breakfast table

Ms. Blake reported back that Karen was getting out of bed with much parental cajoling and reminding, going to the bathroom, washing her face, brushing her teeth and taking off the top and bottom of her pajamas. She was getting five of the eighteen tasks done in a half hour – less than thirty percent of the required chores. And this slim accomplishment was done only when Mom nagged constantly. When Ms. Blake came into Karen's room and discovered she'd only removed a part of her pajamas, she immediately harangued her daughter for not moving fast enough, "I can't believe you've only got half your pj's off and you've been up fifteen minutes. Get on the stick, Karen, or you'll be late. You're such a pain. Why can't you just hurry up?"

Karen would often answer, " I'm going as fast as I can. I don't want to go to school anyway. You can't tell me what to do. Stop yelling at me!"

Ms. Blake and I got busy designing a positive system to improve things for Karen. The mother decided to call the program *Ringing in the New*. Instead of only noticing what Karen hadn't done, Ms. Blake was to instead focus on noticing the tasks Karen had completed. When the mom checked on Karen every three to five minutes, Ms. Blake was to praise Karen for each of the tasks she had completed. Along with the praise for working hard at each accomplishment, Karen got a special piece of purple construction paper cut in the shape of a bell. Purple was her favorite color. Karen got one token - a purple bell – for each of the eighteen tasks she accomplished. Mom sometimes would even ring a bell congratulating Karen for her accomplishments. Since social reinforcement is the weakest form of reinforcer, pairing praise with tokens strengthens the power of the praise so that eventually the tokens can be phased out for many children. We want them to learn to eventually praise themselves for their good effort and keep at it.

Mom reminded Karen of the treats that were in store for her if she got her grooming chores done on time. She could choose to have her favorite breakfast, French toast. She could watch her favorite morning cartoon show on television, or she could take her portable CD player to the bus stop to listen to her favorite music waiting for the bus. Notice Ms. Blake was not reminding Karen of what punishment was in store or the fun activities she'd miss out on if she dawdled too long. She focused on the success she was sure Karen would have and the fun things she'd be doing soon as a result of her quick dressing and grooming.

On the first day of the program, Karen earned twelve tokens at the end of a half hour. She'd done more than twice the tasks from before that were involved in getting ready. She hadn't brushed her teeth so she couldn't choose French toast for breakfast because it has sugar in it. She was allowed to watch five minutes of her favorite cartoon after she finished tying her shoes and brushing her teeth. The cartoon time would have been longer if she had accomplished more of the morning routine on time. Mom didn't belabor the point. She only said, " Look at you! You were able to get five minutes of television time because you got dressed quicker this morning. You are really learning to be such a big girl by concentrating on dressing. As soon as you finish with your shoes and teeth, the TV goes on. Tomorrow I'll bet you'll get even more TV time. Good for you for getting faster. I think I'll ring the bell again just for you."

The next morning fifteen of Karen's chores were done on time. The French toast was savored with gusto as Karen basked in all the praise Mom and Dad heaped on her. She even ran up and brushed her teeth a second time and brushed her hair after breakfast. By the next day Karen was fully dressed and groomed in plenty of time to eat a leisurely breakfast and watch her favorite show. Her proud parents reminded her often of how grown up and responsible she was proving to be. All the while Karen was seeing herself in a totally new light. Instead of viewing herself as bad, lazy, and "a pain," Karen was starting to see herself as a pleasant, helpful, responsible person. The parents had successfully separated the behavior from the child. She now saw herself as a good kid who occasionally dawdled.

The feedback she was getting from her parents was changing her concept of herself to something entirely different than before. Building success into her life had the powerful result of Karen's viewing herself as capable and confident. Her grades in school even improved because now she brought to school a picture in her mind of herself as successful whereas before she had come to school angry, rushed, and hurt from all the put downs she had suffered at home.

Once, weeks later, Karen had resisted going to bed, so she had a hard time getting up the next morning. She slept through the alarm clock. She piddled around all morning and only got herself half dressed, receiving too few tokens to earn any activities or food she liked. Reminding Karen that her bedtime would be a half hour earlier that night, Mom handed Karen her shoes and a muffin and walked her to the bus. Unable to eat the muffin and put on her shoes at the same time, Karen had to hurry to the bus stop to sit on the ground to tie her shoes then start her muffin. When the bus came Ms. Blake waved happily to the tearful Karen. Mom did not exhort Karen or say anything negative. She let the experience teach Karen, rather than lecture the child. Our children rarely truly follow our teachings through to our lectures. Indeed they know the lectures so well they can recite them word for word, so obviously the lecture is not doing the job. Otherwise, since the lecture is known by heart, the lecture should have changed the behavior. What we parents say doesn't change things; what the environment does changes behavior. "Talk less. Act more," is a good motto to remember.

We change our behavior which changes the behavior of our children. Having to suffer the embarrassment of appearing at the bus stop half dressed serves as more of a teaching moment than lecturing or driving your child to school in the comfort of the family car when dawdling has caused the child to miss the bus.

But what worked even better to produce lasting change was the systematic, immediate, and consistent positive reinforcement Karen received for changing her morning habits to being focused on getting ready for school in a brief amount of time. You see, a buildup of negative memories gives us a world view of pessimism. If we choose to notice what our friends, spouse, children and others do that pleases us, we help create a world view of optimism. When people hear that they are appreciated for their talents and skills and the acts they perform that contribute, they repeat these acts and develop an opinion of themselves as loved, competent, and contributing. It's amazing how the whole home atmosphere changes in families once parents start noticing what they appreciate about their children rather than focusing on what they do wrong. It can be catching. Spouses sometimes start to thank each other for the things they might have earlier taken for granted.

I remember after we'd been using the positive reinforcement system at home for a few months, one late afternoon my husband bounded in the kitchen exclaiming, "Your son is trying to shape my behavior. Ty just told me how much he appreciated my repairing his bike and thanked me for grilling outside for dinner." It seems that my kids had noticed all the positive comments we were making and decided to give some back.

David Learns to Contribute

Ten-year-old David never helped out around the house. In fact, he considered it an affront to his dignity to be asked to pick up after himself. He expected his mother to pick up his toys, books, clothes, towels, and food waste after him, He put her down vigorously if she wasn't quick enough in her cleaning up after him. He saw himself as the anointed prince of the household. Mrs. Smithey was getting fed up and resentful toward a ten-year-old child who viewed his needs as far more important than hers. It didn't help that Mr. Smithy also left everything for Mary to do. After attending my six-week *Pennington Positive Parenting* course, the Smithey's were able to agree on several things: David was no longer to be allowed to put his mother down, he and dad were to clean up after themselves, and David must earn his privileges by contributing to the family.

The family had a meeting with the parents setting forth the new rules to David. They set up a *token economy* system - also called an *operant conditioning* plan - in which David earned poker chips for each chore he did around the house. Such a system is often called *behavior modification*, too. He also earned an extra chip for doing a chore without complaining and by refraining a half hour from putting down his mother. Extra chips were awarded for any compliments he gave his mother. He had to earn each privilege through this token system. He earned time on the computer, television time, video game time, sleepovers, and time playing with his favorite toys – his Spiderman action figures. He was asked if he could come up with a better plan. He could not. His complaints that this was unfair fell on his mother's and his father's deaf ears. The family wrote out a contingency contract as a result of this meeting. They continued to have weekly meetings with a rotating chairperson. The agenda was posted on the fridge and anyone could add to it all week. The rule was that even if David was the chair, the meeting was to start and end with each person telling each family member one thing they appreciated about the other.

David was now expected to pick up after himself and to vacuum the living room floor. He learned to set the table and clear it as well as to load the dishwasher.

At first he had a hard time adjusting to the new expectations since he had had ten years to get used to being ruler of the roost. He did not relinquish his throne lightly. When he was first told that he would have to earn television time, he tried to watch TV anyway. This is non-contingent reinforcement and cannot be allowed if a new behavior is to be taught. When he did try to do a fun activity without earning it, he was immediately put in Time Out in the corner of the dullest room of the house – the dining room. If he kicked and hit on the way to Time Out, Mrs. Smithey only counted the hits and kicks aloud so that he would know that one minute per hit or kick was to be added to the ten minutes he would serve in Time Out. A good rule of thumb for Time Out that is considered mostly standard in the field is one minute per year of age. I taught Mrs. Smithey how to grasp David's hands behind his back and march him in front of her to Time Out to prevent his hitting or kicking her. If he refused to stay in the Time Out chair, he was matter-of-factly told that it seemed he had chosen the more restrictive Time Out and marched in the same manner to the laundry room. There the timer was started over. If he stayed in the room, the door was left open; if he tried to leave, the door was shut and even locked. Time Out means no one looks at you and no one talks to you. The Smithey's were good at ignoring all his screaming and swearing. They let him know from the beginning that the timer would start when he was quiet. As soon as he stopped for a minute to catch his breath, they started the timer. If he kicked the wall, he was required after Time Out was over to do a procedure called <u>over correction</u>. This means he had to use a sponge to "clean" three times as large an area as he had kicked even if no marks were on the wall. This was a two-trial learning for him, because he hated having to clean up after himself to begin with. He refused to do the clean up at first, so a hand-over-hand method was used so that his hand was guided by his mother's hand.

Within a week, David was well on his way to becoming the model citizen and family member. He enjoyed all the praise and positive attention he received from both his parents. He was quite accomplished at not leaving his things lying in the family room. He loved turning in his points to get regular and special privileges. Now he truly was in charge of his life, but no one else's.

David had been told early on in the system that he would get points for cleaning up after himself, so now it was worth his while to do so most of the time. He was also told of the logical and natural consequences of leaving his things lying around the common areas of the house. When he would occasionally forget and leave his things lying around the house, Mrs. Smithey would not nag, complain, or mention it again to him. If his things were still lying around at 8:00 P.M, the message was that those items were not important or valued by him.

Having an uncluttered house was important for the family, so the de-cluttering work had to be done by someone. If a person doesn't clean up after himself, he needs to hire a maid to do it for him and pay the maid for the work. Things left out after 8:00 P.M. meant the person had hired Mom as his maid. Her "maid's fee" was fifty cents per item. All items picked up by the "Maid Mom" were put in the Saturday Impound Box. The articles could not be retrieved until Saturday and only by paying the fine. Entreaties that the science book was really needed were ignored. Such logical and natural consequences put forth by Rudolph Driekurs in his book, <u>Children the Challenge,</u> can be very effective in helping children take responsibility for their things. The parent doesn't nag or lecture, but lets the child suffer the consequences of his behavior. If your things aren't important enough to pick up, you lose the privilege of using them for a while and pay a fee to have them picked up by someone else. Just like life.

If we leave our car parked too long, cluttering up a street or parking lot, we suffer the consequence of having to pay someone to haul it away and its being impounded. One expensive impound usually teaches people to be more responsible with their belongings. Any attempts to bypass the impound time or fee at home should be met with a Time Out. If an adult scaled the fence of the impound lot for his car, further loss of his car and money or time in jail would ensue.

Within a month, David was busy picking up after himself and doing several chores to contribute to the family. He loved the system and enjoyed exchanging tokens for activities that he could now count on. He was becoming more pleasant to be around daily. All of us like our lives to be predictable, and David's life had now become so. He knew that if he did what was expected of him, he could bank on being allowed privileges and activities he wanted to do. He eventually looked forward to chairing the family meeting on a rotating basis Sunday evenings. He was seeing that mutual respect indeed went both ways. Parents' allowing him to use his newly discovered leadership ability served to afford him practice and improvement in treating parents with respect.

One of America's most prestigious universities found a real gem of wisdom in a study several decades ago. Research at Harvard University found that the best predictor of successful adulthood was the amount of meaningful work done by a person in childhood. Adult success is not so much related to intelligence, good grades, good schools, or an abundance of expensive toys. We assign chores to our kids and they might complain bitterly. Those chores, those daily jewels of contribution to the household, those daily measures of cooperation toward the common good, are stepping stones to achievement in the grown-up world. It is in those little ways that we daily demonstrate we are hard-working, cooperative and contributing. Here is where we learn that a good measure of who we are is the sum total of the deeds we do for ourselves and for the common good. We learn little by little that we can take care of ourselves and others if need be.

I had my own baton-twirling school at age eight. I charged a quarter per lesson at recess for teaching other little girls to twirl baton like me when I performed as the majorette mascot for our local high school band. Later I earned dance lessons in a studio apprenticeship. Owning my own dance studio by age sixteen allowed me to earn money toward college to offset some of the expenses not covered by the academic scholarships I won. Such meaningful work at an early age besides my home chores taught me the self reliance and joy in living that shapes my days even today so many decades later.

The work of Ivan Boszormenyo-Nagy in Contextual Therapy has found that individual happiness can only be found through fair and just relationships with the people we care for. This can be translated to mean that we are helping our children toward happiness - even though they may complain at the time – by assigning chores in which children contribute time and energy to the family. By not expecting them to contribute to fair and just relationships in the family, we could be robbing them of ego strength and happiness. Some parents do chores for children long after the time they are perfectly capable of doing them by themselves. By being a servant to kids, we do them a dis-service. They never get to see that they are capable of hard work and effort. They never get to see visible proof of their contribution to family life. We give far too many material things to our children hoping this will make them happy. It never does. A sense of contribution, gratitude, and giving back builds the foundation of happiness.

An overall happy mood appears to develop early in life. Our neural set points of mood are not changed in the long term by winning a huge monetary windfall or suffering a devastating loss. Dr. Gerald Edelman found that within a year we all return to the same level of sullen or happy mood as before. Research has also found that the set point for joy in life for animals and humans appears to be the amount of nurturing received in our early years. Letting our kids know about our unconditional love early and often is absolutely important for their later capacity for happiness. Unconditional love is essential. However, this does not mean freedom from responsibility or work in childhood.

When I think back to my childhood, it was my family's poverty and my parents' expectation that everybody had to contribute that were the keys to my hard work to earn several college scholarships for academic merit and to work hard to keep them. My family of origin's poverty gave me few alternatives for my future. I learned a work ethic. I learned gratitude for all that my parents had sacrificed for me. These developed my drive to succeed. The smiles and praise from my parents for my diligence early on rewarded my hard work at home and school. I gained a sense of happiness and purpose. It was up to me to work my way out of our scanty income to later give myself and my own family a few more choices than my parents with their fifth-grade schooling ever had.

Sally Learns to Get Better Grades

Sally was failing eighth grade because she forgot to bring home her homework assignments and books. Even if she did the work, she usually forgot to bring it to school or forgot to turn it in. Things had been sliding downhill for several years. She was discouraged as were her parents. Her teachers were frustrated. She often lied to her parents saying that she didn't have homework that night even when she did. When she finally turned in late homework, so many points were counted off, that her grade was still in the failing range. Even though she was bright, she seemed lazy and unmotivated to achieve good grades and get into a good college. Her room was also a total mess. She spent most of her time drawing, chatting on line, listening to music or hanging out with her friends. The Roth's withdrew Sally from dance lessons and gymnastics so she could devote more time to her studies. She had refused to practice either one at home, so the loss wasn't much to her. When asked why she didn't do her homework, she just shrugged an "I don't know."

My testing found her to have Attention Deficit Hyperactivity Disorder: Inattentive Type. The parents did not want to use medication, so they pursued the only other proven research-based option: a token economy. My written psychological report allowed the parents to get an extra set of books at home for her through Section 504 of the Rehabilitation Act of 1973. Soon forgetting her books could no longer negate her ability to complete her homework. After some training with me, the Roth's set up a sign-off system for Sally's homework.

In a family meeting it was decided that Sally was to write down her homework assignments in her school agenda. Each teacher was asked to initial only if the notation of the assignment were correct. Sally got a point for each teacher initial. This is called a *gateway* item in that Sally was allowed to do a fun activity that afternoon or evening *only* if these particular points were earned. She could earn points for other things such as getting her other homework done, but she was not allowed to trade her tokens in for an activity unless she earned the points for each teacher sign off. We had decided that the parents' knowing what homework Sally was to do was essential to improving her grades for the time being. If a teacher's initial on her assignment sheet were missing, Sally was still required to do work in that subject anyway for a half hour. The parents assigned the lesson from the next chapter in her textbook, some brief research on line, or having her read in an encyclopedia and write a report.

Sally was expected to estimate how much time it would take her to do each assignment. She was to set a timer and if her work completion matched the estimate within a two-minute margin, she got a token. Each quarter hour she spent working on her homework she also earned a token, thus her effort and perseverance were reinforced. The estimation of the time it would take her to do each task improved her time management skills considerably. Now she realized that she often thought she could do a task in a shorter amount of time than was really necessary. She got a token for each correct portion of her homework she completed. She earned daily and weekly activity reinforcers for staying on task and correct work completion.

Sally wasn't expected to make A's in math, her least favorite subject. She was offered tutoring if she wanted to improved her understanding of math concepts that stumped her. Her hard work at mastering these difficult concepts was praised and reinforced with tokens.

Her grades went from D's and F's to A's and B's. She had proven to herself and her parents and teachers that she could be the smart, productive student they had thought she was. Without the option of lying, that behavior disappeared. As her effort and her productivity improved, tokens and praise were given less frequently and less consistently. The sincerity and the truthfulness of the praise remained. Sally started to define herself as hard working and diligent. The tangible tokens – poker chips - were changed to points on a chart as she needed a less enriched reinforcement schedule.

Not wanting to foster dependence, we continued the program until Sally had a whole semester of good grades and no missing homework. We then changed it to teacher reports only once per week. Later reports every two weeks came home from school. Then monthly reports were expected. She was told that any lying about homework would be a message that she needed more supervision again. The system was gradually phased out after several months of intermittent reinforcement to keep the persistence and other new behavioral habits continuing. A few years later she graduated high school with honors.

Mom Teaches Kevin to Control His Temper

Kevin was a ten-year-old boy who also had ADHD, only his was the Combined type involving distractibility, impulsivity, and hyperactivity. He also had the diagnosis of Oppositional Defiant Disorder as well as a Generalized Anxiety Disorder. He had gotten into the very bad habit of screaming at his parents, particularly his mother. He threatened her life almost daily, but he often said he didn't mean it sometime later. Occasionally he apologized, but more often than not he never apologized for yelling such awful things at her as, "I hate you and wish you were dead!" Tantrums were an everyday occurrence. The mother attended my parent training course and learned how to set up a particularly powerful token economy.

With awareness being the first step to change, Ms. Corder first counted Kevin's tantrums daily by keeping a tally on the fridge. When Kevin asked what she was doing, Mrs Corder told him she was keeping track of his temper outbursts. They diminished once he knew she was keeping track of them. Next she started the behavior modification program. Before the intervention he was throwing a tantrum about four times a day. He reduced his tantrums to three the next day, then down to two per day. The next week he only lost his temper and yelled at her once per day. Meanwhile Mrs. Corder was giving him a poker chip for each hour he could refrain from yelling and screaming. As she gave Kevin his token, she said," You've managed you emotions well for an hour. I appreciate how hard it is for you." If he handled an event well that in the past had precipitated a tantrum, he got a bonus token. The second week after the program started, he had no angry outbursts. No outbursts! Zilch! He was seeing tangible proof in the charts she was keeping that his effort at improved self control were paying off.

Because the mother was careful to be SHIC (Specific, Honest, Immediate, Consistent) with her praise, Kevin was starting to get used to a new view of himself as respectful, polite, and cooperative. The mother learned how to assertively ask for change from him. She put her request for fewer threats and hate messages in the form of an <u>I-message</u> instead of a message about how rude his behavior was. She said, " When you tell me you hate me and wish I were dead, I feel so hurt, unimportant, and disrespected. I don't deserve that from you. I need you to talk to me in a respectful manner. Will you please stop and think about what you are saying to me? Think about how you would feel if someone said those things to you. If you will treat me with respect, I will continue to treat you with respect. But if you treat me with disrespect, I won't have the good feeling necessary to give me the energy to do many of the favors you tend to expect from me such as driving you to the mall or to ball practice.

Mrs. Corder had successfully used the assertive <u>I-message</u> she learned. This way of communicating is a way to stop being a doormat and stop taking emotional abuse but not lashing out aggressively toward someone you'd like to see change. The middle point between Human Doormat to Human Volcano is assertiveness in which you ask for your needs to be met without attacking the other person. It is a way of communicating with others on an equal, human to human basis.

It goes like this:

<u>I- Message or Assertive Communication</u>

a. When you_____.

b. I feel_____.

(Be careful not to talk about how mad you are so that you only get anger back. Also it's best to stay away from the words "like" or "that". If you use these, you've flipped into a thought rather than a feeling. It works only if you stay with one or two words describing how you are feeling.)

c. I need_____.

d. Will you_____?

e. If you will, I will_____.

Through these messages to Kevin of how his behavior really effected his mother, he was finally able to start to develop some empathy, an essential social skill. Empathy is a key ingredient of emotional intelligence - an ability that contributes much to a successful life in adulthood.

The next time that Kevin exploded toward his mother with his threats of violence I made him do a **<u>Real Apology</u>** to her in my office. This intervention has proven very successful in changing severe behaviors that are antisocial such as threats, stealing, cheating, lying, and aggression. It is another tool I use to help my patients with poor impulse control and anger management problems develop empathy. Sometimes the victim is not available to come to my office so the parent who has brought the child there is the recipient of the first apology because the parent has always suffered some emotional distress when the child has victimized others. If the other victims are not available to sit down with the perpetrator in my office, the child remains in his room except for bathroom, school, and meals until his other apologies are written and read to the victims. Amends must also be made before the perpetrator is released from his confinement. This method forces the perpetrator to witness the devastating effects his behavior has on others, apologize to the victim and develop a plan to make amends and a plan to improve future behavior.

If the victim is not there, an apology letter must be written with all the right components and read to the victim. The perpetrator must also do some behavior that is a gesture toward making amends. I require the perpetrator to look the victim in the eye and go through the steps of a **<u>Real Apology</u>**:

REAL APOLOGY

Remember it's not over until the hurt person believes you and forgives you.

*Here's what I did that hurt you:*_____

(Specific acts must be named.)

*Here's what I was thinking at the time:*_____

(An answer of "I don't know" or "I wasn't thinking" is never accepted. The answer is usually something like: "I thought I could get away with it."

*Here's what I was feeling at the time:*_____.

*Here's how the person I hurt must have felt at the time:*_____.

(Child must ask the parent if he can't think of anything but anger. There is usually worry, disappointment, sadness, hurt, and distrust underneath all the anger. These must be acknowledged and voiced.)

*Here's why I shouldn't have done it:*_____.

(A reason more than suffering punishment must be given.)

Here's how I am truly sorry: _____.

(Child must convince the parent that he truly regrets having done the misdeed.

*Here's how I plan to make amends:*_____.

(Some concrete action must be done to save the other person energy or time or the perpetrator makes a gift of his time and/or money to the other person.)

*Here's my plan to make sure I don't do it again:*_____.

(Just saying "I won't do it again" is not enough. Specific steps in a plan must be written out and memorized. The plan must begin with "The next time I start thinking and feeling like this, I will: ....)

FEELINGS LIST

abandoned	confused	exhausted
excited	impressed	skeptical
barely adequate	condemned	fearful
agonized	contented	flustered
inspired	overwhelmed	solemn
ambivalent	contrite	foolish
intimidated	pained	sorrowful
anxious	crushed	frantic
isolated	panicked	stupid
apathetic	deceived	frightened
jealous	pleased	startled
ashamed	defeated	full
jumpy	pressured	stunned
astounded	delighted	free
kind	proud	suffering
awed	despairing	glad
left out	refreshed	sympathetic
betrayed	different	gratified
lonely	rejected	tempted
bewildered	discontented	guilty
loved	unloved	unimportant
relaxed	tense	threatened
bold	distracted	happy
loving	relieved	tired
bored	disturbed	heavenly
melancholy	remorseful	trapped
brave	dominated	helpful
helpless	miserable	restless
troubled	burdened	divided
homesick	mystified	reverent
ugly	calm	doubtful
honored	neglected	rewarded
uneasy	capable	incapable
unappreciated	appreciated	challenged
ecstatic	terrified	disappointed
innocent	nervous	satisfied
unsatisfied	charmed	electrified

horrified	hurt	dull
odd	stressed	obnoxious
scared	uneasy	cheated
empty	irrational	nutty
settled	unsettled	wonderful
cheerful	enchanted	oppressed
weepy	embarrassed	energetic
shocked	worried	childish
envious	lost	silly
clever	smart	put down
discouraged	encouraged	enthralled

Refer often to these when you are using your new-found communication skills.

The token economy, assertive communication from the mother, and a **Real Apology** were effective tools to getting Kevin on track to a better life. At last meeting, his outbursts had totally disappeared and he had become much easier to live with. His school had noticed a more cooperative, attentive youngster. Kevin was a much happier, friendlier person than before.

JIM LEARNS TO TAKE RESPONSIBILITY

Sixteen-year-old Jim had failed ninth grade twice and was headed for his third failure of that grade. He rarely remembered what his homework assignments were and even more rarely actually did them. His parents had taken him out of league football and his grades had removed him from his high school football team. He had lived for football and now it was gone. He was depressed, feeling he had nothing to live for. He would sneak out at night trying to spend time with his girlfriend. The parents had grounded him from contact with her for a month after his violating curfew when he was with her. He had become very disrespectful to both his parents. He had been known to go into fits of rage that had landed him in a psychiatric hospital more than once.

My testing found Jim to have ADHD: Combined Type as well as Oppositional Defiant Disorder. (A note to parents, if a child is failing a grade, it is time to ask questions and find out why.) Testing found his academics to be on grade level. It was his effort that was lagging. He did not have a learning disability.

We tried a token economy first before trying medication, because I have found that if families try medication first, they think they have a cure and the other necessary treatments are ignored. In a family meeting, a program was set up in which Jim earned all his privileges and activities. Jim had to have each teacher initial his notation of the correct assignment for that night. These initials earned him free time at home. His homework time was divided into half hour segments. He earned tokens – points on a chart – for concentration and correct work completion. He earned tokens once per hour for refraining from treating his parents disrespectfully. The accompanying praise went something like this, "Good job. You're concentrating so you're getting it done and done correctly. I appreciate that you're being respectful, too." He also earned extra tokens for any time that he did or said something pro-social, cooperative and contributing at home. Note that the appropriate behavior is described in the praise, not the behavior that he was not doing.

Daily he exchanged his tokens for time on his cell phone or the family phone to talk to his girlfriend. Each day that he displayed an attitude of helpfulness and respect was a day knocked off his month-long grounding from seeing his girlfriend. He started to do his chores and homework fast and well. His grades improved dramatically.

Between his grades improving and his helpfulness at home he also earned weekend privileges of using the family DVD player and computer to go on-line. He also was able to earn the use of the family car on weekends by being appropriate and displaying a cooperative, respectful attitude.

Three years later I was thrilled to get a graduation announcement in the mail!

Wynn and Ty Learn to Cooperate With Each Other and Reduce Quarreling

My sons, Wynn and Ty Pennington, are twenty months apart in age. Until they were in high school, my budget was so tight that they had to share a cramped bedroom. At ages seven and nine, they fought and argued constantly. After I got Ty's behavior under control at school with a token economy, I next focused on helping them to learn to be together without the bickering that took place daily.

I told them in a family meeting that henceforth they would get a token every half hour or so that I noticed they were not quarreling or fighting. I had to set a timer to remind myself to go and find them in order to give them praise and a token. If I saw either of them doing or saying something that was particularly nice to the other, I presented that boy with a "Caring Coupon", worth five tokens. They were already using an activity menu to spend their tokens, so an extra five points was a big deal to them. It could mean an extra five minutes playing a board game with me that evening or other reinforcers off the menu we had drawn up as a family.

My own awareness exercise had shown me that I rarely mentioned to them my pride when they were getting along well. I had just expected them to get along without my prompting, encouragement, or praise. I shouldn't have been surprised that ignoring their good behavior together did not produce any friendlier interactions than what I had seen between my brother and me when we were growing up. Things got so bad between Donnie and me that we didn't even speak to each other at school. I considered him a juvenile delinquent and he saw me as a goody two shoes. As adults we are now friends, but I wish we could have learned some better interaction skills way back then.

The token system allowed Wynn and Ty to experience a different way to be together rather than the constant "me first" mind set so many siblings get into. At first they were so sickeningly sweet to the other, it almost made me gag, but new habits were being laid down. I made sure that I reinforced the event of saying or doing something nice to a brother and going so many minutes without quarreling. This is **event** sampling as well as **time** sampling. I was careful not to give a token to either of my sons if he told me of some compliment he'd paid to his brother. I knew by then that would be reinforcing asking for a reward, rather than reinforcing the caring behavior itself.

The token system didn't cure their fights forever. They'd still get into arguments sometimes, but not nearly as often as before. The rule became that if they did choose to fight, they'd not earn a token for that half hour. Tokens were not taken away. Each kid knew that he could count on keeping the reinforcement he had already earned. Each was punished with Time Out for physically fighting. Each always had the option of leaving the room to avoid punishment for fighting. I no longer would come to their room to solve their quarrels, since I was beginning to see that these situation were often a play to get my attention.

Consider changing complaints into plans for change. Rather than, "I can't get my child to stop making a mess," try, "I must devise a plan to teach my child to do the small, specific steps required to pick up after herself."

If the complaint is, "My child won't do a thing I say," try making a prescription for change such as, "I'm making a plan to teach my child to comply with reasonable adult requests. I understand my part in the behavior and promise myself to change my behavior."

Rather than "My kids are at each other's throats all the time," we could make a plan for change, "I will teach my children different ways to be with each other by reinforcing and praising each step along the way with SHIC praise (Specific, Honest, Immediate, Consistent).

CHORE LISTS AND APPROPRIATE AGES – Start one at a time

Two years: Pick up toys after self

Three years: Above plus empty small trashes around house, put own clothes & towels in hamper.

Four: years: Above plus taking own dishes to sink after meals.

Five years: Above plus helping fold laundry. Hanging up jacket & clothes.

Six years: Above plus making own bed, putting clean clothes in drawers, packing book bag nightly for school, simple yard work such as picking up stones and sticks.

Seven years: Add cleaning own room, sorting, washing, and drying own clothes in machines after practice and supervision. Dusting furniture. Setting table and clearing it. Preparing snacks. Folding and putting away family laundry. Write thank-you notes for presents.

Eight years: Add vacuuming, cleaning bathrooms, wiping table after meals, feeding and watering pets.

Nine years: Add planning and preparing family meals with supervision. Loading & unloading dishwasher. Doing family laundry. Raking or blowing leaves. Open own bank account and add to savings regularly.

Ten years: Add sweeping and mopping kitchen, bathrooms, porches, decks. Add cooking simple meals for family. Wash windows and pictures. Help vacuum and wash car. Empty garbage, roll to street and return.

Eleven Years: Add cleaning baseboards, dust mopping under beds, cleaning garage, yard work. Helping with spring cleaning.

Twelve years: Add planning and cooking more elaborate meals without supervision. Helping with clerical work of bill paying except for signing checks. Wash and vacuum car alone.

Thirteen years: Add community or charity work, regular savings of part of earnings from odd jobs in neighborhood.

Fourteen years: Add regular meal preparation without supervision. Simple home repairs under supervision.

Fifteen years: Add regular car care and cleaning. Responsibilities are done without parental reminders. At least two days a week has dinner ready for family when working parents arrive home.

Sixteen years: Earns gas money if using family car. Contributes money to car repair and maintenance.

Questions and Homework for Chapter 4

1. The first step in designing a behavior change project is to develop _____.

2. Pairing praise with _____ strengthens the power of praise so that eventually _____ can be phased out for many children.

3. Significant improvement in behavior happens when the focus is on _____ rather than failure.

4. What we parents _____ doesn't change our children's behavior so much as what the environment does to change their behavior.

5. Parents can teach lasting changes in behavior using systematic, _____, and _____ positive reinforcement.

6. When a child gets a reward without doing the required work, it is called _____ reinforcement.

7. The procedure requiring the child to put things back better than they were before is called _____.

8. Successful natural and logical consequences are best imposed by parents who don't _____, _____ or lecture.

9. Parents should talk _____(more/less. Circle one), act _____(more/less), listen (more/less)_____.

10. To design an "I message" you first _____.

11. In an "I message" when describing your feelings, you avoid the words _____ and _____.

12. In describing your feelings, you avoid saying how angry you are. You also avoid

80

using other words that are synonyms for anger such as

_____.

Design an "I message" for someone in your family, practice it silently for a few times. Fill in the blanks, write it, then deliver it.

13. When you _____.

    I feel _____.

    I need_____.

    Will you _____.

    If you will, I will_____.

14. Write a **Real Apology** for something you as a parent have done that hurt or worried your child or spouse even though you may not have known it a the time. Be sure you spell out specifically what you did. Report what you were thinking and feeling at the time. Write how the other person must have felt when you did it. Describe why you shouldn't have done it and how you're truly sorry. Develop a plan to make amends and do it. Write your plan to make sure it doesn't happen again._____

_____

_____

_____

_____

_____

_____

_____

_____

_____

_____

Read the apology letter to the person who needs to hear it and give it to them so the two of you can checkup on the plan once a week for a while.

15. Start your behavior change project designed in the last chapter. Target only one or two behaviors at a time.

16. Go back to the list of chores expected by ages of children and circle off the chores your child is expected to do to contribute to the running of the household. Start to bring your child up slowly to age level by adding one chore at a time after you get the first target behavior under control for a few weeks.

17. What is the pay off for one of your behaviors, your spouse's behaviors, or your child's behaviors. (If there were no pay off, you wouldn't keep doing it.) Write that behavior and the payoff here.

_____

_____

answers:

I. awareness II. tokens, tokens III. success IV. say V. consistent, immediate VI. non-contingent VII. over-correction VIII. nag, yell IX. less, more, more. X. describe the behavior XI. like, that XII. upset, frustrated, mad.

82

CHAPTER FOUR

MY PLAN FOR IMPROVEMENT

My plan for showing my understanding and improving my positive interaction with my family is:_____

The way I'll know it's working is::_____

I will do these less: call names, threaten, punish, interrupt, resent, act as maid, etc,
_____.

I will do these more: apologize, listen, show understanding, share responsibility, use logical and natural consequences, expect contribution, use fairness, communicate assertively, pay attention to the emotional life of my family, make time for fun, remember to be SHIC with my praise, etc_____

My specific plan is"

Monday_____

Tuesday_____

Wednesday_____

Thursday_____

Friday_____

Saturday_____

Sunday_____

Fill out this page, photocopy it, and carry it with you daily.

CHAPTER 5

MORE TIPS FOR DESIGNING AND IMPLEMENTING SUCCESSFUL TOKEN ECONOMIES

> **Be Aware of Developmental Limitations**
> **Limit Discouragement by Limiting Response Cost**

When Todd was six and in first grade, his teacher designed a behavior change project to keep him in his seat and not disrupting class. Every time he misbehaved she put a mark by his name on the chalkboard. Five marks meant he got a note sent home for misbehavior. The parents diligently punished him at home when he got a bad note, which was very frequently. He earned a smiley face stamp on his hand at the end of the day if he had stayed seated and done his work. Nothing changed in Todd's behavior except that he got more and more frustrated with himself and the teacher because he never was able to last a whole day without getting out of his seat. He never got his hand stamped. To Todd this was daily proof that he was bad and stupid.

Teachers often tell me they have tried a token economy and it didn't work. Of course it won't work if it is poorly designed. There is no such thing as a bad child, only a bad behavior management system that can be corrected. Let me repeat: **There is no such thing as a bad child, only a bad behavior management system!** I believe we are all born innocent, full of self esteem, joy, and curiosity We are born eager to please and eager to learn. Often the environment teaches us otherwise. The environment taught Todd that he was a trouble maker and not worthy of any praise or kind words. He could only look forward to public humiliation with his name on the board if he continued to do what seemed to be his natural bent.

I urged the teacher to try true operant conditioning – reinforcing the appropriate behavior immediately and consistently. She was to divide the school day into segments of about a quarter to half hour each. She was to use a timer to remind herself that it was time to check in on Todd. Every quarter hour that he was seated and reasonably quiet, he got a check mark on a small chart he brought in his pocket from home daily. The check mark was delivered by the teacher at his desk with a hearty, "Good job, for listening so well!" and a pat on the back. I taught her about SHIC (Specific, Honest, Immediate, Consistent) praise. Fifteen minutes or so was all the time he could pay attention to his work. For a boy his age with his poor attention span, waiting a whole day for reinforcement would only result in failure.

Some children have even shorter attention spans. In second grade, my son, Ty, was observed to have an attention span of ten seconds. This was the intensity of the enriched reinforcement schedule he required to succeed. I designed an token reinforcement system to keep him in his seat and working. It turned his life and his self concept around from "trouble maker" to a boy who was contributing, hard working, competent, and caring. The full story is on the companion *Pennington Positive Parenting* DVD to this book

The day that reinforcement was delivered at Todd's developmental level, he started to achieve. If his behavior was not very disruptive, his teacher learned to ignore Todd for that short time period. As soon as he was seated and back to work, she could pile the praise and points back on.

Once seen as the list of shame, the names on the board became a competition for

"Kid of the Day" award. Any time the teacher noticed a child being especially appropriate, she put a check mark beside the child's name on the board. She made sure that Todd's name got a few checks beside it daily. He took his pocket chart home daily and earned daily activity reinforcers from his parents for his much improved behaviors at school.

When so-called token economies don't work, I invariably find that there is inconsistent reinforcement that is not immediate, but reinforcement that is far removed in time. The steps are far too high for the child to be successful. I also find that the back-up reinforcement is usually not powerful enough or frequent enough to motivate the child to change.

I discourage making the child suffer for minor misbehavior in the beginning of a behavior modification project. These are best ignored. The question of taking away points also comes up. I discourage that, too. I believe in letting the child keep the points he has earned unless the child tends to be oppositional a lot or defiant. In that case he will probably require his tokens being taken away, known as <u>response cost</u>.

My bias against taking away tokens came from my experience as a psychologist in a special center for behaviorally disordered adolescent males. Often in the mornings these boys would come to school with a chip on their shoulder because of something that had happened at home. A boy would make a smart remark to the teacher and she'd fine him some points. The teen would then get even more belligerent resulting in the loss of even more points. Within five minutes he would have lost a week's worth of tokens he had previously earned for good behavior. By that time, he was feeling hopeless, enraged, and he was throwing things. Often the police had to be called before the episode was over. If the rule for the teacher had been to only fine once, then use Time Out or isolation for punishment after that, such a catastrophe would have been avoided. By the way, it turned out that almost all these boys originally only had ADHD, but it was never diagnosed nor treated appropriately. By the time I encountered the boys, each was headed straight for jail. Many studies have been done documenting the very poor adult outcome for ADHD without continued effective multi-modal treatment, most recently Russell Barkley's work reported out at the national CHADD conference in Chicago, October, 2006. Compared to others, adults with ADHD have poorer driving records and are much more likely to end in fatalities. Their work lives and personal relationships are dramatically fraught with failure compared to normal peers.

It is imperative that we get more diagnostic help and effective treatment to these kids and other kids who are struggling who might have this disorder, but have not been diagnosed. One very effective intervention is a well-designed token economy. So, if the child doesn't do well on the token system you have devised, modify it so that he can be successful. Give tokens more frequently, more immediately, and more consistently. Give more powerful activity reinforcers more frequently. To make something grow make sure you water it liberally and frequently with praise and other types of reinforcement.

Make Sure You Reinforce What You Want to Strengthen Rather Than Another Behavior

Alex was sucking his thumb long after it was developmentally appropriate. He was four. His mother wanted to use positive reinforcement to change things. She started praising him every time he took his thumb out of his mouth. She soon noticed that he was sucking his thumb even more. Can you figure out why? He had to put his thumb into his mouth before taking it out, so the more he sucked his thumb so he could take it out, the more praise he got. What would have been a better way? You were right if you answered that she should praise him for any length of time he kept his thumb out of his mouth.

Dad tells Marcia to load the dishwasher. She refuses. Dad says, " I'll give you fifty cents if you will." Is this a good way to get youngsters to be cooperative and contributing? No, it trains them instead to refuse to help because the promise of a reward came right after the refusal. Remember behavior increases if a reward comes right after it. This is the mistake many parents make thereby training their kids to refuse to work without a reward. It is the root of many complaints I hear about using operant conditioning when parents have inadvertently trained the kids to be beggars and refusers.

When I do social skills groups for kids, I have a lesson on compliments. Giving compliments to others is one of the a marks of a socially competent person whom others like to be around. It's an important skill for each of us to learn. When I tell the kids in the group that from now on I will give bonus points each time I notice anyone giving a compliment to his neighbor, immediately I start hearing a barrage of compliments toward others from each member of the group. Within minutes if I am not quick enough to notice a compliment by a group member, he'll invariably ask, "Dr. Pennington, I told Robert I liked his shoes. Do I get a token?"

My answer is always, "No." If I were to give that youngster a token, what would I be reinforcing? Asking for a reward, rather than the behavior I'm trying to increase. The kids protest a little at first, but they get used to it quickly and realize that I will notice most of their pro-social behavior, but I will miss one occasionally. This way the kids learn to compliment others rather than to ask for rewards. At the beginning of a behavior management project, it is best to tell children that if they ask for a token, it will not be given. Also tell them that if they refuse to do a chore without a token, the token will not be given, but the chore must still be done or they must face logical consequences.

You Can Have Your Cake and Eat It, Too

I encourage parents to allow kids and teens to exchange their tokens for an activity reinforcer daily. As a matter of fact the usual thing that makes a behavior modification program fail is that too few reinforcers – both token and activity - are given too far apart. I like to see parents start out with allowing a child to trade in some tokens each day. Insist that at least one token be exchanged daily. For younger children even a twice a day trade is needed. The child's progress can be monitored on a chart, and if he's had more than half good days all week he should get an activity reinforcer on the weekend. The rule could be that he spends the left over tokens not spent daily for a weekend activity. A weekend activity menu is used, otherwise all weekend activities can be lumped into one menu without assigned values

Weekend reinforcers are usually easy to come up with: movies, DVD's, trips to the park, breakfast at a fast food restaurant, and having friends over among other things. It's the daily activity reinforcers that are hard to think up because of the limited time available during the typical school week. I encourage parents to ask their youngsters what rewards they'd like to earn each day. I assign parents to list five new daily reinforcers appropriate for their child's age group. The reader is to circle those that are appropriate for your age child. Then mark the daily ones with a "1", The weekly activities to be earned mark with a "2", the monthlies with a "3", and the quarterly ones with a "4". Here is a *sample* list which is by no means exhaustive :

_Bake somethings

_Make popcorn

_Play with paper cutting box

_Bike riding with/without Mom

_Popsicle after dinner

_Backyard ball toss with Dad

_ 15 Min. of Play-Doh with Mom

_Paint a picture

_Dance together

_Play on the tire swing

_Go swimming

_Polish nails

_Read an extra story

_Half hour video games

_Picnic in living room floor

_Have a circus play house

_Work in basement with dad

_Make pudding

_Make snow cones

_Blow bubbles

_Badminton

_Go out to lunch/dinner

_Play in the creek

_Card game with Mom

_Board game with Dad

_Hide and Seek with Mom

_Go for a walk with Dad

_Go fishing

_Play Simon Says

_Sing together

_Play with kid's makeup kit of cast offs

_Make a tent in the living room

_Make a scrap book house

_Call friend on phone

_Jumping Bull Ride on Dad

_Do a puppet show

_Make a video

_Work in the craft box supervised

_Play Blind man's Bluff

_Sleep outside in tent

_Bubble bath with bath foam

_Call Grandma

_Chair the family meeting

_Use "Special" plate/ place mat

_Cartwheel contest with mom

_Cook hot dogs in fireplace

_Day with Mom/Dad at work

_Make hot cocoa from scratch

_Tickling with mom

_Jogging with dad

_Biking further than regular limits

_Make a birdhouse with dad

_Finger paint or paint by number

_Melt crayons and paint with them

_Play musical chairs with family

_Take photo of family

_Play electric trains with dad

_Do arts and crafts

_Declare a "Backwards Hour"

_Print a digital photo

_Work with tools under supervision

_Play Sling Statue with Mom

_Stay up late a half hour

_Choose family television for half hour

_Get " Kid of the Day" Certificate

_Play with walkie-talkie with Dad

_Get to eat one meal with your hands

_Use the cell phone a half hour

_Light candles at dinner

_Wrestle with Dad

_Have a friend over for dinner

_Ice cream parlor visit

_Calisthenics or treadmill with Mom

_Jump on miniature trampoline

_Weave a pot holder

_Construction paper, glue, markers

_Whole family eats meal with fingers

_Make an activity scrap book

_Have a silly hat party at home

_Teach Dad "cool" lessons

_Plant a window garden

_Put stickers on your toes

_Dress up in costumes with parents

_Start a tree house

_Jump in a pile of leaves

_Splat Mom with shaving cream pie

_Make art stamps out of potatoes

_Choose dinner menu

_Cut cookies into shapes

_Write name in noodles on paper

_ Lead a family parade

_Make baking soda/vinegar volcano

_Make balloon animals

_Play a comb and tissue kazoo

_Assigns family seats for dinner tonight

_Sleepover

_Extra goodies at movie

_Download from I Tunes

_Chair family meeting

_Trip to another state

_Driving supervision with Mom

_Have a scavenger hunt

_Solve a mystery with hidden clues

_Horsey ride with Dad

_"S'mores" night in fire-pit

_Make a card for your cousin

_Build a fort in the living room

_Throw a wet sponge at waterproof Dad

_Get a temporary tattoo

_Be Family Boss for 10 minutes

_Help cook dinner

_Skip all way around outside of house

_Have family guess what you invented

_Play a toy drum for 10 minutes

_Make a pipe cleaner animal

_Learn a magic trick

_30 minutes of computer time

_Rent DVD

_Trip to theme park

_Use of iPod

_Trip to beach

_Write a play and film it

_Trip to Aquarium

_Trip to go cart track

_Pillow fight

_"Easter" egg hunt in July

_Piggy back ride with dad

_Trip to nearby town, mall

_Leather working   _Chore-free day

_Video arcade with $ _Music lessons

_Baseball cards   _Bake clay figures you've made

_Rock climbing   _Horseback riding

_Supervised driving   _Use of special computer software

_Watching *Extreme Makeover: Home Edition* :0))

Contingent Versus Non-contingent Reinforcement

Some parents have a hard time deciding how to use activity or monetary reinforcers when a child has his own money. A teen who has a job has disposable income, making it much more difficult for the parents to use contingent reinforcement. If the child/teen can still do the desired activity, such as buy or use the coveted electronic gadget, he is receiving non-contingent reinforcement. No behavior change will take place under these conditions.

It is perfectly reasonable to insist that the child's money be in a joint account with you. After all, you are furnishing all the logistical and other support to allow him to have a job and earn money: food, shelter, and clothing to be exact. Usually parents provide the transportation to the job as well. Assure the youngster that the dollars are still his, but access to the money will be contingent on his behavior at home, particularly treating family members with respect and having a good attitude. Such good citizenship behaviors are critical for later success. Teens need to practice them at home. These kinds of rules are particularly important for a teen with an oppositional defiant disorder. This type of child is argumentative, picks verbal fights with people, is disagreeable, defies authority, and resents parents and teachers having the audacity to tell him what to do.

If the teen balks at these rules discussed in a family meeting, one alternative is to charge the teenager room and board. Check around and find out how much rental rooms in homes cost in your area. In other words, if he is using family resources, he needs to be contributing by doing chores and having a respectful, appropriate attitude. This way he can be earning points daily for the weekly privilege of using the family or his own car for weekend fun or using the iPod nightly.

Use of the family car is a privilege not an entitlement. If he has to pay most of his money for room and board, but probably not quite as much as it would cost on the open market, he will be more likely to abide by the family rules and treat parents and other family members with respect and cooperation.

We parents must ponder how we learn to make it in the real world. Remember the hard lessons of finding out how much things cost when you were a young adult or late teen? The sooner kids learn the value of time and money, the more likely they will become successful adults. Do not allow disrespect in your home. Make that disrespectful kid earn every privilege. Give him points for effort, cooperation, contribution, and a respectful attitude.

More About the Teen Scene

Know that negative behaviors are learned and your teen is bright enough to unlearn them and replace them with pro-social behaviors. Even the attitude of teenagers can be unlearned and re-taught. Parents must remember that SHIC praise can help and can go a long way. Remember the parts of SHIC?

Write them here now: S_____, H_____,

I_____, and C_____.

It is so tempting to do this, but we need to especially remember not to add a "zinger" at the end of our praise. "Your grades came up this semester, why don't you change your attitude once in a while?" Such praise gives with one hand and takes back with the other. We need to add another rule about praise, particularly for teens. The praise should also be un-contaminated or un-muddied with negative comments so that the overall message is negative. Now our mantra of our mnemonic is USHIC:

Uncontaminated

Specific

Honest

Immediate

Consistent

Teens require daily tokens, but often by this age, the tokens are points on a chart, rather than the tangible tokens such as poker chips that younger children require. My son Ty, even as a teen, required hourly tokens in school in the form of teacher initials on a slip he brought in his pocket daily to school. He got the point each class period all the way through high school for attention to task in class. Many teens may not need such an enriched reinforcer schedule by the time they get to middle or high school. Since ADHD kids are laboring under a slower developmental timetable behaviorally, emotionally, and with a younger attention span, they may need such support for their efforts much longer than teachers or parents are likely to want to give it. Teachers will argue that he's too old to be babied this way. The truth is that if he were developmentally ready to handle it on his own, he would already have it mastered.

The activity reinforcers we might have used for younger kids, no longer have the same appeal to a teen. Now it is all about their friends and peer group, which is developmentally appropriate. A teen's daily reinforcers now will be more about use of electronic gadgets, use of an iPod, or cell phone. Time on the cell phone with friends is a big reinforcer for a teen. The weeklies will be more about time with their friends and use of the car. It is especially critical for teens that we reinforce effort and steps along the way. These steps along the way are <u>successive approximations</u> toward the final behavior. Don't wait until he is the star of his own television show before he gets a word of praise for his efforts. 10% percent of *something* beats 100% of nothing any day of the week.

Logical and natural consequences can be very useful rather than the use of Time Out or <u>response cost</u>. Consider these behaviors and the appropriate logical and natural consequence. Add your own at the end.

LOGICAL AND NATURAL CONSEQUENCES

BEHAVIOR	*CONSEQUENCE*
teen leaves bike out in the rain	loses bike privileges for a day
teen leaves clutter in family room	maid's fee and impound box
teen misses curfew by half hour	½ hour earlier curfew next night
teen refuses to get off computer	loses computer use next day

teen doesn't do his kitchen chores	loses kitchen privileges next meal
teen brings home car empty of gas	loses car privilege next day
teen goes to bed ½ hour late	_____
teen late to school	_____

Parents of teens should pay particular attention to the chapters in this workbook that describe <u>I-Messages</u> or assertive communication, contingency contracts, reflective listening and a <u>Real Apology</u>. You will probably not use Time Out so much as response cost once, then isolation, and logical and natural consequences.

How to Keep the Behavior Going

After a behavior is well established for several weeks, switch to intermittent reinforcement to make the new behaviors stick. You must still keep giving tokens and praise every once in a while to remind the youngster that he is still expected to keep up the new habit.

The necessity of this became apparent years ago when I was working with a family whose nine-year-old ADHD son – we'll call him Tommy – was also encopretic. He pooped his pants several times a week, but would hide the evidence way back in his closet or under his clean clothes in his chest.

I helped the parents set up a token economy to address the problem. Years later I learned that ADHD kids are more prone to this disorder than other kids because they are less likely to spend the necessary time sitting on the toilet. What happens is that fecal matter gets impacted at the sphincter and relaxes that muscle. Liquid matter above the impaction makes an end run around the impacted matter and leaks out. Since the sphincter is so relaxed, not as much feeling is there, so often the child doesn't know he's had a runny B.M. Such a disorder is known as occult constipation, because everyone would swear he's not constipated because he seems to be going all the time. Occult constipation is treated with enemas, laxatives and regular trips to the john with some minutes sitting there. I didn't know any of this back then, so I tried behavior modification.

Since the accidents never seemed to happen at school, Tommy was called in from playing outside every half hour or so after school and on weekends. His pants were checked. When they were clean – and they always were once the program started, he was given praise, a token, and a reminder to go sit on the john for a few minutes. John sitting was also reinforced with a token and praise.

If his pants were clean all week, the family got a trip to the ice cream store on Sunday night. To the delight of the whole family, Tommy cured his dirty pants problem. It worked when his play mates' harassment and teasing hadn't. His brother's calling him nasty names such as "Closet Crapper" only had served to embarrass him more and make matters worse. The baby sitter making him "moon" the city bus one night hadn't helped either, he just got better at hiding evidence as long as punitive measures were used. The parents screaming at him when the dirty pants stash was found also only made his self esteem plummet further. It was only when what he was doing right and well – noticing Nature's call and sitting on the toilet at the right time – that Tommy was able to kick the problem and start to feel good about himself.

After the behavior had been eliminated for several months, the parents stopped the program. Within a week, Tommy was back to his dirty business of pooping his pants.

The parents were starting to have a "poopy" attitude about life and Tommy until I reminded them that the rule about switching to intermittent reinforcement had been ignored. Of course the behavior had returned.

They reinstated the program. This time they called him inside intermittently. Sometimes it was once per afternoon. Sometimes it was several times a day. Often a day or so was skipped. At the end of the week two slips of paper were placed in a hat. One had the word, "Yes" on it, the other, "No." Tommy drew out of the hat if he had had a perfectly clean week. Sometimes he'd draw the "Yes" slip which allowed the visit for ice cream. But the "No" slip ensured that no ice cream would be eaten even if he did have a perfect week.

Dr. Robert Cloninger found the place in a rat's brain that monitors the reward center in the brain. It's located in the orbital and medial pre-frontal cortex. This center switches on when there is lack of immediate reward and tells the brain to keep up the effort, that reward is coming. He found that rats learn persistence when they are not rewarded every time. Translating to humans, this means that when we switch to intermittent rewards after a behavior is learned, we are training folks to not expect a reward every time.

Such is life. Las Vegas makes billions annually on the principle of intermittent reinforcement. They know that to keep a behavior going – customers feeding slot machines – every so often some prize money must be awarded. Please remember not to stop your token system cold but rather taper down to intermittent reinforcement to keep the new and improved behavior continuing. This way you can train your child that he can make it through frustrating times with persistent effort.

Guidelines for Modifying Behavior of Children

- Reward appropriate behavior frequently with praise, activities, or tokens immediately and consistently. Use praise that is honest, specific and un-contaminated by negatives.

- Make sure your reinforcement is positive.

- Enlist your children's help and cooperation with contingency contracts.

- To eliminate or reduce a behavior reward the incompatible or opposite behavior.

- Ignore minor infractions that are not connected to the target behavior.

- Reward small steps toward the eventual goal.

- Sometimes prompt the response you want to ensure success.

- Don't cloud the praise with "but." Be loud and clear with praise.

- Make sure the target behavior is observable. Pinpoint one or two behaviors at a time. Don't overwhelm him.

- Structure the situation initially so that inappropriate behavior is less likely to occur.

- Make sure the reinforcers are valuable to the child and only obtainable through performance of the target behavior.

- Clearly state the rule, positively and briefly. Write it down, and both parent and child sign it. Make sure you stick to the rule, too. Modeling is the best way to learn or teach.

- Learning takes place much faster with positive reinforcement. There is more carry over to other situations and less avoidance tactics than if punishment is used.

Combination often needed with impulsive and/or defiant children,

- With younger, more impulsive children, more frequent changes in the reinforcers are required.
- Some kids require restating the rules often. If he is punished, he must state the rule he broke. Child can also earn tokens for being able to state the rule before misbehaving.
- After a behavior is established, switch to intermittent reinforcement to keep it going.
- Rewarding appropriate behavior is not bribery. Bribery is rewarding illegal or immoral behavior. Operant conditioning offers incentives for appropriate behavior in adults and children.

SOME EXAMPLES OF USHIC PRAISE

I really like the way you listened just now.

You are getting better and better at sticking to it.

I know this is hard, but you are working hard to solve it.

You've tackled hard things before and succeeded. I see you working hard at this one, too.

You've been creative in the past coming up with solutions, I notice you're putting in the same effort now.

I loved the way you helped your little brother get dressed just now.

You really contribute to the family when you load the dishwasher the right way.

I know that learning to be respectful is breaking old habits for you that have been around for a while. I appreciate how hard you're working on changing your attitude.

I appreciate how focused you've been the last hour on studying for that science test. You seem to know the material now from your hard work.

Your work cleaning the garage makes such a huge improvement in this space. You've really shown how focused you can be when you're on a roll.

Add your own here:

_____
_____
_____
_____
_____
_____
_____
_____
_____
_____
_____

Review and Homework for Chapter 5

1. Initially token economies fail when reinforcement is not _____ nor _____.

2. Taking away tokens is called _____ and is usually _____.

3. At the beginning of a behavior change project, minor misbehavior is best _____.

4. If a child asks for a reward or refuses to do task without a reward, a reward should/should not (Circle one) be given.

5. Make a list of five daily activity reinforcers that are appropriate for your child's age: _____
   _____
   _____

6. After a behavior change has been well established, switch to _____ reinforcement to keep it going.

7. Reward _____ steps toward the eventual goal.

8. Effective praise to teach a new behavior should have these components:
   U_____, S_____, H_____,
   I_____, C_____.

9. Continue your behavior change project and reward yourself for sticking to it.

answers: I. consistent, immediate II. response cost, discouraged III. ignored IV. should not VI. intermittent VII. small VIII. uncontaminated, specific, honest, immediate, consistent.

CHAPTER FIVE

MY PLAN FOR IMPROVEMENT

My plan for improvement in my independent action rather than just reaction and my new direction in family relationships is_____

The way I'll know it is working is _____

I plan to do less of these (circle all that apply): punish, nag, lecture, react, lose my temper, allow non-contingent reinforcement, etc,_____

I plan to do more of these (circle all that apply.): praise, reinforce immediately, improve consistency, catch them being good, use tokens paired with praise, praise that is USHIC, etc_____

My specific plan is:

Monday_____

Tuesday_____

Wednesday_____

Thursday_____

Friday_____

Saturday_____

Sunday_____

Complete this page, photocopy it, and carry it with you daily.

CHAPTER 6

"NUTS AND BOLTS" TOOLS FOR SUCCESSFUL

BEHAVIOR MODIFICATION PROJECTS

*Any of the following charts and other tools may be photocopied for the reader's use. Furthermore, you have available a downloadable and printable companion workbook filled with all these forms. You can find it at http://www.ypsychology.com/downloads/ppp/ipworkbook.zip and the password to open it is **PPPIPWorkbook** (Note, the password is case sensitive).*

Here is an example of a contingency contract worked out in a family meeting. It is best to be very specific and write down the agreement so that later the document can be cited. Be sure the child and parents sign it. I have used these with children as young as three years of age. It is very useful with teens.

Contract for Improvement

Date_____

I, _____, promise to_____
_____
_____.

If I work hard at this, my parents will _____
_____
_____.

_____ (Name of counselor, tutor, relative) can help by_____
_____.

The logical and natural consequences that will result from breaking the contract are _____
_____.

We will meet again to discuss progress on _____.

Signed_____(youth)

_____(parent)

_____(witness, helper, parent)

Football Score Card

1 touchdown = _____ points a day
1 game won = _____ points a week
1 season won = _____ points a month

Rewards to Exchange for Touchdown: (Each has different point value)

1 balloon
1 soft drink
1 candy bar
1 ice cream bar
Choose family TV for ½ hour
1 comic book
1 chance in grab bag
15 minutes alone with Mom, Dad, or teacher
1 good conduct badge to wear for the night
Use bath foam in bath
Skateboard for half hour
Mom tickles you
Others:_____

Rewards to Exchange for Game Won (Each has different point value)

Have friend sleep over
Trip to park with dad
Breakfast at McDonald's with mom
Waffle breakfast from dad
Zoo, putt-putt golf
Skating trip
Movie
Others: _____

Goals	Mon	Tues	Wed	Thurs	Fri	Sat	Sun
Daily Totals:							

This is the program I used for my son, Ty Pennington, starting in second grade. Before I started this system, Ty spent almost every day in the principal's office. The day before I started this program was the last day in his school career he was sent out of class. Learn more about how this system worked with the accompanying DVD of one of my actual *Pennington Positive Parenting* workshops. I've done this workshop for more than thirty-six years with pre-treatment and post-treatment behavior rating scales. If parents do what I teach them, things get dramatically better. One of these slips was in Ty's pocket every school day. Every half hour through third grade, the teacher initialed his score card. Later it was initialed only once per hour. After conduct was licked, we switched to a work completion score card.

CONDUCT SCORE CARD

Teacher, please initial the appropriate place if student has behaved reasonably well for the period.

1st Period _____   4th Period _____

2nd Period _____   5th Period _____

3rd Period _____   6th Period _____

CONDUCT SCORE CARD

Teacher, please initial the appropriate place if student has behaved reasonably well for the period.

1st Period _____   4th Period _____

2nd Period _____   5th Period _____

3rd Period _____   6th Period _____

CONDUCT SCORE CARD

Teacher, please initial the appropriate place if student has behaved reasonably well for the period.

1st Period _____   4th Period _____

2nd Period _____   5th Period _____

3rd Period _____   6th Period _____

CONDUCT SCORE CARD

Teacher, please initial the appropriate place if student has behaved reasonably well for the period.

1st Period _____   4th Period _____

2nd Period _____   5th Period _____

3rd Period _____   6th Period _____

WORK COMPLETION SCORE CARD

Teacher, please initial appropriate space if the student has completed ____percent of expected work for that period.

1st Period _____   4th Period _____

2nd Period _____   5th Period _____

3rd Period _____   6th Period _____

WORK COMPLETION SCORE CARD

Teacher, please initial appropriate space if the student has completed ____percent of expected work for that period.

1st Period _____   4th Period _____

2nd Period _____   5th Period _____

3rd Period _____   6th Period _____

WORK COMPLETION SCORE CARD

Teacher, please initial appropriate space if the student has completed ____percent of expected work for that period.

1st Period _____   4th Period _____

2nd Period _____   5th Period _____

3rd Period _____   6th Period _____

WORK COMPLETION SCORE CARD

Teacher, please initial appropriate space if the student has completed ____percent of expected work for that period.

1st Period _____   4th Period _____

2nd Period _____   5th Period _____

3rd Period _____   6th Period _____

HOME MANAGEMENT SYSTEM

GOALS	Mon.	Tues.	Wed.	Thurs.	Fri.	Sat.	Sun.
Follow directions							
Neaten up							
Pleasant to family							
Get permission							
Solve problems							
Chores on time							
Other:____ _____							
Totals							

Name_____ Week_____

HOME MANAGEMENT SYSTEM

GOALS	Mon.	Tues.	Wed.	Thurs.	Fri.	Sat.	Sun.
Follow directions							
Neaten up							
Pleasant to family							
Get permission							
Solve problems							
Chores on time							
Other:____ _____							
Totals							

Name_____ Week_____

Daily Responsibilities

Morning	Mon	Tues	Wed	Thurs	Fri	Sat	Sun
Up by ___ w/ alarm							
Grooming: face, hair, teeth x 3							
Pick up after yourself							
Dressed by ___ & in kitchen							
Family manners							
Afternoon	Mon	Tues	Wed	Thurs	Fri	Sat	Sun
Pick up							
Agenda initialed							
Homework completed in 1.5 hrs							
Book bag packed							
Chores: dusting, laundry, trash, etc							
PM/Bed	Mon	Tues	Wed	Thurs	Fri	Sat	Sun
Kitchen jobs							
Family manners							
Bed prep by ___							
Bed by ___							
Other:							
Totals							
1 point per	15 min	tasks	15 pts = 50	Cents.	After-school	Activities =	15 pts required
	Mon	Tues	Wed	Thurs	Fri	Sat	Sun

FREE TIME MENU
WHAT I LIKE TO DO

If I could do anything I wanted for a half hour, I would choose:

- Call my best friend on the phone
- Call grandma
- Ride my scooter
- Play hopscotch
- Play army
- Cook mac and cheese in the microwave
- Make popcorn
- Roast marshmallows in the fire pit
- Soak in the hot tub
- Other:_____
  _____
  _____
  _____

Circle the ones you like the most.

How many points should each cost?

WHAT I LIKE

The things I like to do after school are
_____.

If I had $5.00 I would
_____.

My favorite game is
_____.

My favorite TV program is
_____.

I like these sites on the web
_____.

My best friends are
_____.

My favorite CD is
_____.

My favorite toys are
_____.

I love to make
_____.

My favorite books are

_____.

My favorite animals are

_____.

The places I like to go in town are

_____.

The two things I like to do most are

_____.

My hobbies are

_____.

My favorite activities outdoors are

_____.

Use this to find out what rewards your child is most likely to work toward.

Graph of Behavior Change

Improvement in _____'s _____ behavior

DATES: _____ to _____

M Tu W Th F Sa Su M Tu W Th F Sa Su M Tu W Th F Sa Su

M Tu W Th F Sa Su M Tu W Th F Sa Su M Tu W Th F Sa Su

Graph the days of the week across and the percentage of the behavior occurrences out of possibilities on the vertical with 5 % increments up the left side.

Permission is granted to photo copy this and other charts. Each behavior should be separately charted.

121

Mom's/Dad's Graph of Own Positive Statements to Family Members
Baseline Before a Behavior Modification Project

DATES: _____ to _____

M	Tu	W	Th	F	Sa	Su
M	Tu	W	Th	F	Sa	Su

Parent should try to be as accurate as possible as to counting the number of positive exchanges before starting the family makeover.

Positive Statements Made By Parent
After Starting Behavior Change Project

DATES: _____ to _____

M	Tu	W	Th	F	Sa	Su	M	Tu	W	Th	F	Sa	Su	M	Tu	W	Th	F	Sa	Su

M   Tu   W   Th   F   Sa   Su   M   Tu   W   Th   F   Sa   Su   M   Tu   W   Th   F   Sa   Su

Set up a reinforcement system for yourself for each daily and weekly improvement in number of positive comments. Ideas: golf, lunch out, hot tub soak, massage, appreciation note from spouse, guilt-free pass from home chores for a day, fresh-cut flowers, take out meal, home-cooked favorite meal, night out with the boys/girls.

AWARD
FOR MOST IMPROVED KID
OF THE WEEK

This certificate is presented to _____

for significant improvement in _____.

This award is to acknowledge all the hard work that went into this dramatic change. Your diligence is greatly appreciated.

Signed_____

Date_____

This certificate entitles the bearer to _____,

redeemable on _____.

KEEP UP THE *GOOD WORK!*

Cut these statements out and paste them inside the cupboard, on the dash, on your bathroom mirror. They can help you remember to get out of your criticism habit we get into so often. Change them often so you are more likely to notice them. Use whatever you can to break the negative cycle.

SPRINKLE *LIBERALLY* WITH PRAISE

QUICK, PRAISE HIM BEFORE IT'S TOO LATE

DESCRIBE WHAT YOU LIKE

ABOUT WHAT SHE'S IS DOING

IF YOU WANT TO GROW SOMETHING,

WATER IT WITH PRAISE

CATCH THAT KID BEING GOOD

GROW SOME CONFIDENT KIDS TODAY!

NOTICE ANY STEPS

TOWARD IMPROVEMENT

STOP YELLING AND BUGGING

AND START HUGGING

Nice Things We can Remember to Say

I'm so glad you're here. You contribute a lot when you finish your chores on time.

Thank you for being who you are. I see your caring when you help with dinner.

I appreciate all the caring things you do. Like right now, you're folding laundry. Thanks.

I want you to know that I notice your kindness. That was sweet of you to share your cookie with your sister.

I love how creative you are. You work hard at figuring out new ways to do things.

That is great listening.

You have worked hard to develop your talent for music,

I'm so proud of how hard you're trying. Math used to be hard for you, but your concentration has paid off.

You are so unique. What a great idea you just had.

There's no one quite like you. That kitchen counter looks so clean.

I really appreciated your help today. Your attitude was helpful, too.

Thank you for being quiet so Mommy could get a nap. That's being a good citizen.

You can be quite the big brother. Thank you for holding your brother's hand.

Good for you. You weren't sure you could sound out that word, but you worked at it and you did it!

I just love how playful you are. How about a high five.

You're funny. Give me a hug.

I like hanging out with you. You are so pleasant to be with.

You have such a pleasant disposition today. Good for you for making that choice.

Wow! That's a clean room!

You're learning every day better ways to be helpful.

Thank you so much for all the effort you put into that project.

Add your own here:

_____
_____
_____
_____
_____
_____
_____
_____
_____
_____
_____
_____
_____
_____
_____
_____
_____
_____
_____
_____

APPLICATION AND HOMEWORK FOR CHAPTER 6

1. Circle several ways you intend to use to encourage yourself to stay more positive than negative

    Set up reward system for yourself.

    Tell your spouse you appreciate his/her efforts to change.

    Ask for the same from your spouse.

    Use a timer to remind yourself.

    Post signs around as reminders.

    Carry tokens with you so they' re handy.

    Call friends for support and tell them of your successes.

    Take a picture of you and/or your child smiling and post it on the fridge.

    Set yourself a quota to give out so many token daily – say 40.

    See tokens as little love notes to your child you might not remember to send otherwise.

    Set small goals at the beginning to ensure success.

    Remind myself that no parent is 100% great.

    Remember that if I keep my intention to continue my improvement, great things happen.

    Remember to use USHIC praise for yourself, too.

2. Continue your behavior change project, chart it, and pat yourself on the back for doing it. Share your success with a friend.

CHAPTER SIX

MY PLAN FOR IMPROVEMENT

My plan to improve my planning and integrated action is
_____

The way that I'll know it's working is
_____

I plan to do less of these (circle all that apply): nag, punish, lecture, yell, interrupt, criticize, etc, _____

I plan to do more of these (circle all that apply): notice improvement, USHIC praise, be consistent, immediately notice good behavior, use several different types of reinforcers, remind myself of the gains made, take time to bond, connect, play, etc, _____

The specifics of my plan are:

Monday_____

Tuesday_____

Wednesday_____

Thursday_____

Friday_____

Saturday_____

Sunday_____

Complete this page, photocopy it, and carry it with you daily.

CHAPTER 7

PHYSICAL, SOCIAL, AND PSYCHOLOGICAL UNDERPINNINGS OF ADHD AND WHAT TO DO ABOUT THEM

What's ADHD Anyway?   Is This a Real Disorder?

I've been doing a presentation for about twenty years on the diagnosis of ADHD called, "What Looks Like a Duck, Sounds Like a Duck, Walks like a Duck Could Be a Duck." I have a poor, benighted volunteer come out of the audience and proceed to dress the person up progressively like a yellow duck. I present the poor soul with several feathers, which represent birds of a different feather that are not really ADHD. I help the person don a yellow cover as he starts to look possibly like the duck we're considering, ADHD. He exhibits the classic behaviors: he's distractible, impulsive, and can't be still very long. Here's the actual official list of behaviors. Like with a Chinese menu, you can **pick six of the first nine for inattention**.

- often has difficulty sustaining attention in tasks or play activities
- often fails to give close attention to details or makes mistakes in schoolwork, work, or other activities
- often does not seem to listen when spoken to directly
- often does not follow through on instructions and fails to finish schoolwork, chores, or duties in the workplace (not due to oppositional behavior or failure to understand instructions
- often has difficulty organizing tasks and activities
- often avoids, dislikes, or is reluctant to engage in tasks that require sustained mental effort (such as schoolwork or homework)
- often loses things necessary for tasks or activities (e.g. toys, school assignments, pencils, books, or tools)
- is often easily distracted by extraneous stimuli
- is often forgetful in daily activities

Then pick six of the nine for hyperactivity-impulsivity:
   First for hyperactivity:
   - often fidgets with hands or feet or squirms in seat
   - often leaves seat in classroom or in other situations in which remaining seated seated is expected
   - often runs about or climbs excessively in situations in which it is inappropriate (in adolescents or adults, may be limited to subjective feelings of restlessness)
   - often has difficulty playing or engaging in leisure activities quietly
   - is often "on the go" or acts as if "driven by a motor"
   - often talks excessively

   These are the official symptoms of impulsivity:
   - often blurts out answers before questions have been completed
   - often has difficulty waiting his turn
   - often interrupts on intrudes on others (e.g, butts into conversations or games)

Symptoms must have been present before the age of seven, be present in at least two settings and offer signs of significant impairment in academic, social, or occupational functioning for some time. The symptoms must not be originating from another disorder. This is the rub. The rule out differential diagnosis. Hence the duck presentation.

First I have to differentiate the child from the normal child, the first bird of a different feather I must take away. The way a good mental health professional does this is with an individual and family history. The fact that this is an inherited disorder that runs in families is the strongest strand in the literature. The use of behavior rating scales that are normed compare this child to his age and sex peers. The parents and teacher complete these. For an adolescent or adult, the patient also completes such forms. For an adult, the significant other can offer much information. A behavior observation in the office or at school can give considerable information. I also use individually administered instruments that measure attention and impulse control. All theses data set the ADHD person apart from the normal person of his age and sex. A feather of a bird of a color is removed so that the volunteer becomes more duck-like once ADHD is separated out from normal for age and sex.

To remove another bird of a different feather, sensory deficits must be ruled out as well as any physical disease. A thorough medical exam is required for this. There are also medical problems that mimic ADHD with the same or similar symptoms such as head injury, delirium, dementia, chronic obstructive lung disease, hypothyroidism, and hyperthyroidism. More medical look-a-likes include renal insufficiency, hepatic insufficiency, and vitamin deficiency.

A psycho-educational evaluation rules out an impaired intellect that could be keeping a youngster from concentrating in class. Thus another bird of a different feather is removed.

A thorough psychological evaluation and history helps the mental health professional rule out situational or family stressors as the culprit. Previous teacher reports will show if this is just a problem in this classroom and with this teacher. A life events inventory will document the life changes the youngster has undergone. Other measures such as a family environment scale will document the family milieu, a parenting stress index will tell you how stressed the parents are. A clinical parental interview helps to answer many of these questions so that you are able to take away another bird of a different feather adding more duck-like features, because this is an inherited, life-long disorder.

The child could be suffering from one of several learning disabilities such as reading or reading comprehension problems. Also, poor math computation or math reasoning or poor expressive language could be keeping him from succeeding in school. For ADHDs the more likely learning disabilities present are in the area of written expression and receptive language. Of course he's not going to follow directions if he doesn't understand them to begin with. Very often part of the struggle with homework could a be a written expression learning disability. With this rule out, another bird of a different feather is taken away as our duck comes to look more and more duck-like. By this time I've added head feathers or tail feathers to my embarrassed volunteer.

Anxiety and depression are the causes for many symptoms that are more or less temporary that could be driving the inattentiveness. Ever been so worried you couldn't concentrate? Of course, but it goes away when the temporary cause of the worry goes away: the test is over. Ever been so depressed after a loss that you can read a whole chapter and not have the vaguest idea what you've read? Yes, but it was temporary and goes away after a few months. Ever been so worried you paced back and forth until your missing pet was found? Yes, but the symptom went away when the stressor was removed. Sometimes we make impulsive, impatient decisions when we're worried. If your husband is hours late getting home from the office and you've heard nothing from him, how patient are you with the children? Not very much, but after the worry goes away, we return to our typical ways of being more on an even keel. Behavior rating scales that look at more than just ADHD symptoms can help the clinician determine if anxiety or depression are part of the problem. Child self report instruments are also useful and can help determine how long these emotional issues have persisted. I use creative expressive techniques such as projective drawings and Sandplay to root out such emotional issues that may be co-occurring or be the true heart of the matter. Thus another bird of a different feather is removed from the volunteer and he acquires a duck-webbed foot.

More disorders that have symptoms that mimic ADHD must be ruled out. Schizophrenia, bi-polar disorder, antisocial personality disorder, borderline personality disorder must be addressed or ruled out. Alcohol and other substance abuse must be examined with an adolescent and adult.

There are also intermittent explosive disorder, dissociative disorders, post traumatic stress disorder, anxiety disorders, obsessive-compulsive disorder, and work or school phobia, although school phobia is now called separation anxiety. All these disorders can produce some of the same symptoms as ADHD. These are addressed in the history through careful questions. If these are not the reason for the symptoms, another bird of a different feather is removed and the volunteer gets another duck foot.

The difficult problem with differential diagnosis is that many of these disorders can be co-morbid or occur at the same time with ADHD.

The final rule out of another bird of a different feather is the usual pejorative terms the typical ADHD person has been called all his life: lazy, willful, stubborn, unmotivated, not trying. This problem is addressed by individually administered measures of attention and organization, done when total attention is present. Anecdotal records and formal observation procedures can lend more credence to the fact that these symptoms may be coming from a brain that works differently than others. If these issues are ruled out, the final bird of a different feather is taken away, and a duck noise maker is given to my volunteer. Then we see that what walks like a duck, looks like a duck, sounds like a duck is probably a duck and is probably ADHD.

It's often a relief for people to hear that there's a reason for their poor performance and they are particularly relieved to hear that there are very effective treatments available.

Most parents are hesitant to try medication initially, which is why I teach the next best alternative or adjunctive therapy called *behavior modification*.

Physiological Underpinnings of ADHD

Many of the parents who use this book and attend my parenting workshop have children who exhibit the symptoms of Attention Deficit Hyperactivity Disorder or ADHD. The symptoms include distractibility, impulsivity, and/ or restlessness as described above. One can have one, two, or all three symptoms. It is a matter of degree as to whether a child's symptoms are frequent and severe enough to warrant a formal diagnosis of ADHD.

When my son Ty was diagnosed in second grade, his pediatrician did not "believe" in Ritalin, about the only medication used back then. (Of course, now there are many other medications available.) The tests we use nowadays to diagnose the condition were also not available then either. His doctor recommended an EEG, now known to be an in- effective tool for the diagnosis of Hyperactivity, or Hyperkinesis as it was titled then. It was also called Minimal Brain Dysfunction or Minimal Brain Damage (without any scientific proof). Another term used then was Hyperkinetic Reaction of Childhood. Imagine being told your child's brain doesn't work. Imagine trying to tell your child he's brain damaged. So Ty knew he was hyperactive back then, but he didn't know it was a disorder that he had.

The name of the disorder changes every few years as advances in scientific knowledge increase. I happened to be in graduate school for psychology when Ty's life fell apart in second grade. Through use of a token economy that I designed and took to

144

his school, Ty was able to settle down and not live in the principal's office any longer. Indeed the day before I started his token economy was his last trip to the principal's office ever. At first he required intensive in-class help. Later we were able to phase back to reinforcement the teacher alone could handle. Ty's life was turned around for the better through the use of systematic, positive reinforcement of his appropriate school behavior.

My first guinea pig for non-drug treatment of the disorder was Ty. In the years since I have expended countless hours in research, reading, attending professional conferences, and listening to world experts in this disorder. I have consumed many, many hours in deep thought about the basic core problems of ADHD.

Here is my take on the required elements for symptom presentation:
- A organ that is somewhat different (not damaged, not dysfunctional, not disabled)
- An environment conducive to symptom presentation
- An event that comes into the life of every child placing increased demands on coping skills

We now know after more than two decades of research with very sophisticated technology that ADHD folks have something different going on in the pre-frontal cortex of the brain. Some studies have pointed to a developmental lag in maturation as much as thirty percent behind the chronological age. Sometimes there is decreased blood flow to that area of the brain. Many studies have pointed to the lack of noradrenaline and dopamine to fuel the critical receptors in that part of the brain. Just as your car won't work if it doesn't have enough fuel, the pre-frontal cortex won't work well without the fuel it needs.

This part of the brain is associated with screening out distractions and waiting till more data are in before making decisions. Without the proper fuel, these functions won't work to full capacity.

The kind of environment that enhances the likelihood of ADHD symptom presentation is the kind of environment in which most of us were raised and schooled. It is an environment in which what we do that is focused, well thought out, and pro-social is ignored. When we mess up, we really hear about it. This is the regular home and school environment in which most of us live our lives and even create in our own home without realizing it. Research has shown that most teachers in regular classroom give out a ratio of at least three negative to one positive in their comments to their class. Matheny's study even found the ratio to be twelve negative to one positive. These teachers are just normal folks. If we are honest with ourselves, we must admit that most of what our kids hear at home is negative, too.

The third necessary element is school entrance. Before kids start to school, they can run, play, and don't have to adhere very much to schedules. They engage in activities that interest them and that are fun and entertaining. Once school starts, kids are expected to sit, be quiet, and work on mostly monotonous, dull tasks. They must relinquish fun and games for hours at a time in favor of tasks that in and of themselves are not particularly fun or interesting to many kids.

This is my recipe for ADHD symptoms. To make this cake all three ingredients are required. Years and years ago, my uncle was thrown out of school at seven years of age because he kept jumping out the first grade window. Nowadays he would have been diagnosed with ADHD, but psychologists were not around in his small town back then. The laws of compulsory school attendance were not in effect back then either. After expulsion, he was kept at home on the farm, in the barn feeding the animals, and working in the fields. He was not seen as having a problem nor was he seen as overactive on the farm. Problem was that he never got an education and never learned to read or write. A very poor outcome indeed.

Critics who charge that ADHD doesn't exist and wonder where the ADHD kids were a generation or so ago might find the answer by looking at school drop outs and kids expelled from school. Studies have shown that correctional facilities are full of undiagnosed ADHD adults and juveniles.

Often kids who have ADHD tendencies are not seen as problems in early elementary years if they are lucky enough to have very nurturing, positive, structured teachers who might allow a lot of free time early in the day for kids to play and to run off some steam before they are expected to sit for a long period of time. Such teachers keep changing activities frequently and exhibit an enlivened, entertaining teaching style. But such teachers are few and far between. I know I was not such a teacher on most days way back in my teaching career in public school. I do remember the time I tap danced the rhythms of poetic iambic pentameter to my high school English class. They seemed to pay attention more that day, but it was rare that I could come up with such antics to entertain them.

Most teachers have average personalities and aren't nearly as talented and funny as the typical well-paid television star. Our kids would much prefer to be watching cartoons or other entertaining television, but at school they are faced with tasks that require them to sit at a desk all day without getting to play much or run off steam. Of course symptoms usually start to appear upon school entrance when a child is expected to sit for a long time working on fairly dull tasks.

Now about that different brain with the low availability of noradrenaline and dopamine. For years people in my field had talked about the paradoxical effect of stimulant medication on hyperactive kids. It appeared as though these kids had too much of noradrenaline because they were up running around the room so much. Noradrenaline works a lot like adrenaline. It was only in the early eighties that actual research was done to assay the levels of neurochemicals in the bloodstream of hyperactives. It was found by drawing blood several times a day from a group of hospitalized hyperactive boys that it wasn't that they had too much noradrenaline, it was that they had too little. This finding was stupendous and earth shattering in its day.

Think about this scenario. You are on a long, dull highway, straight, with few interesting geographical or botanical features. In Georgia for me it is Highway 16, the one that goes from the center of the state to Savannah on the coast. It runs 150 miles through flat, empty land with nothing but a few scrub pines on the road side. Every time I drive it, I get bored and sleepy. So what do I do? I wiggle in my seat, I turn up the radio, I sing loudly to myself, maybe even slap my face to stay awake. I stop often for a caffeine drink and to walk around a bit. Anything to stimulate myself to stay awake.

A child with ADHD in a dull classroom during a subject that doesn't particularly interest him is doing the same thing: doodling, sharpening his pencil, poking another kid, talking, or looking out the window. He's doing anything to stimulate himself to keep himself more alert because he doesn't have enough noradrenaline available when and where he needs it in school.

Our task to ameliorate these kids' functioning is to use methods known to improve brain chemistry for the better. Stimulant medication is the best researched method of improving brain chemistry for kids and adults with ADHD. Note that I am not anti-medication even though I raised my son Ty without stimulant medication. It can be really helpful for many if not most ADHD kids and adults. Side effects are few and generally pretty manageable.

The only research that I've read that has given me any pause when I suggest to patients to explore efficacy of stimulant medication was done by Dr. Jaak Panksepp at Bowling Green University. He found that stimulant medication given to rats reduced the activity in their brain's area devoted to play. When you think about it, a hyperactive child is full of energy. An impulsive child is pretty spontaneous. A child who moves from one thought to another quickly in play would be seen as distractible in another setting. All these kids would be described as a very playful, but they could also be described as having ADHD. Remember this research has been done only on rats, so conclusions drawn on humans are premature. So far I've not noticed any decline in Ty's playfulness, spontaneity, energy, or creativity on stimulant medication as an adult neither in person when we're together nor on television. He didn't take it as a child so I can't speak to that. I do know that he was given lots of freedom to play at home, and this may have improved things tremendously. There is considerable evidence in scientific research that play improves mental function, emotional function, social skills, and coping skills.

Another way our noradrenaline is increased is through fear. This is why some kids seem to perform better for dads than moms usually, because Dad's voice is lower and stronger, and Dad is bigger than Mom. A mother will report that it will take four hours for her ADHD son to complete his homework, but if Dad comes home and threatens him within an inch of his life, the work gets done in a half hour. I do not recommend fear as a motivating factor in managing children, but increasing the sense of urgency for the work to be done could rev up the noradrenaline to a level that might increase on-task behavior. Use of a timer could help with a race against the clock. Racing another child to get correct completion of a task is another similar idea. Have him estimate the time it will take to do a task, then have him work to try to match his estimate.

Another even better way to improve brain chemistry is regular aerobic exercise. The person must keep his body moving rapidly through space in weight-bearing exercise for at least twenty to thirty minutes. Most sports don't qualify because they involve stop-start-stop-start movement. Imagine how many cases of inattentive children would be vastly improved it the kids ran around the block or building before school, at lunch, and after school before sitting down to homework. I now know that when I required Ty to run around the house several times before sitting down to dinner so that he wouldn't spill his milk so often, I was improving his brain chemistry so that he could focus.

Omega 3 fatty acids found in fish oils are also believed to improve brain chemistry. Such supplements are available over the counter.

It is also known that an environment with an enriched positive reinforcement schedule improves brain chemistry. Imagine that you are at a fun party with friends you like, your team just won the World Series, and you've lost twenty pounds and several people have said you look great in your new outfit. Your brain most likely is producing more noradrenaline and dopamine than usual and you are feeling great. You are focused, making well thought decisions, and able to stay with a group of friends even through someone's rather lengthy, uninteresting story.

This is why my behavior management class has been so effective for so many years with thousands of ADHD patients. The course teaches parents to become reinforcer machines so that their frequent praise and other reinforcement gives their kids a steady boost of noradrenaline and dopamine. The kids bask in all that praise and positive attention and great things happen. The chemical bath their brains receive of these alertness, feel-good neurotransmitters serves as a shot in the arm for self esteem and mood. Such a boost is associated with improved behavior and attitude.

Imagine what the words we hear or say to ourselves are doing to our bodies and our brains. Imagine what the words we say to our children are doing to their bodies, the neuro-chemistry, and the psyches of our kids. Remember when you give a token, activity, or primary reinforcer, be sure and let your child know that you value the contribution he is making to the family. The praise should be heartfelt rather than lifeless and disinterested. We parents are about the business of making a generation of people. They are living, breathing, and – most of all – feeling human beings who need our love, care, and positive attention.

Another hint about appropriate praise – those words that can effect our kids so much more than is evident in the moment. Praise is best given specifically and cleanly. What I mean by this is that is that when kids are told they're angels, and they're not really, they may experience what is called cognitive dissonance. Such an event means that when what a person hears about himself doesn't match what he thinks of himself and what he's used to hearing, he cannot truly believe the new information. Like an orchestra out of tune with each other, with such cognitive dissonance, our kids don't see the new material jibing with the old information. Often their behavior becomes worse. Research was done with kids who were used to being yelled at and put down. When they suddenly heard they were wonderful, they couldn't believe the new in-coming information, so their behavior worsened. How do you fix this? Give specific praise for the particular behavior you see. Praise the process and the effort. Remember to also say, "I'll bet you're proud of yourself too."

The idea of clear, uncontaminated praise is related here, too. What if you were to tell your adult friend, "I love that suit on you. Don't you wish it were a different color?" Your friend would not remember the compliment, only the "zinger" you added at the end. We'd never say such a thing to a friend or colleague, but we do it all the time to kids.

A parent will say, "I really like the way you brought your grades up this semester. I just wish your attitude would change!"

I might say to the parents who attend my workshop – but I never would, "That was a fantastic behavior change project you did. Why didn't you bother to chart it?" Notice how the "zinger" at the end takes away all the good feelings engendered by the compliment. You might as well not even say the nice thing if you're going to take it back immediately after. I hate to keep harping on it, but it is so important. Remember to keep your praise at least at first USHIC:

Uncontaminated

Specific

Honest

Immediate

Consistent

Later you can be less consistent, but the other qualities remain.

If there is something you want your child to improve, wait until another time to tell him so he has this one time to bask in the glory of his accomplishment without contamination. Later you can use an "I-message" to convey your concern about another behavior you'd like to see change. .

Underlying Social and Psychological Issues of ADHD and What to do About Them

I do a presentation about the hidden issues with ADHD kids. I talk about how if there is no diagnosis, the child has no voice so I put a gag on the volunteer who has bravely accepted to play a part in my presentation. I discuss the fact that these kids are unfocused and listen poorly. They might as well have their ears plugged up. I tie a cover over the person's ears. They are so disorganized and impulsive they don't see beyond their noses so they might as well be blindfolded. I blindfold my subject. ADHD kids and adults are often overwhelmed and not much gets done. They may as well have their hands tied. I tie up my helper's hands. I find these kids emotionally guarded because they have had to endure so many blows to their sense of themselves. Since emotions are housed in the body, rather than the head, I tie a band around the person's chest.

After a while of suffering with ADHD issues without effective treatment, self esteem starts to plummet and it becomes hard to stand on one's own feet emotionally. Often folks with ADHD also become depressed. I tie my volunteer's legs together. Frequently the social skills of ADHD folks are poor. They can't reach out to others, so they might as well have their arms tied against their sides. I do that to my helper. Families of ADHD folks get dysfunctional. They get set into rigid roles: usually one overwhelmed parent, one somewhat emotionally distant parent, one golden-haired child who can do no wrong, and one child who is scapegoated. Guess which role the ADHD child plays. You guessed it. The ADHD child is often a lightning rod through which we fight our marital battles and most other family quarrels. I tie a band around the legs of my volunteer – a tough place to be for anyone.

Here is the summary of the typical problems with ADHD youngsters:

SUMMARY OF PROBLEMS AND NEEDS OF ADHD

- UNFOCUSED, LISTENS POORLY
- DISORGANIZED
- IMPULSIVE
- OVERWHELMED
- EMOTIONALLY GUARDED
- LOW SELF ESTEEM
- DEPRESSED
- POOR SOCIAL SKILLS
- FAMILY DYSFUNCTION

If the problems is that the child is unfocused and listens poorly, try these suggestions. If you do, you may might just be able to remove the ear plugs the child has been invisibly wearing.

PROBLEM: UNFOCUSED, POOR LISTENING
NEEDS:
- PROVIDE HELP IN FOCUSING BY HAVING HIM REPEAT BACK DIRECTIONS, PROVIDE FREQUENT BREAKS, LIMIT COMPETING STIMULI
- PROVIDE ENVIRONMENTAL AIDS SUCH SELF MONITORING TAPES, STUDY CARRELS
- TEACH LISTENING SKILLS, ATTENTION, FOCUSING SKILLS, PROVIDE A PRIVATE WAY FOR HIM TO ASK QUESTIONS
- REWARD LISTENING, FOCUSING, ATTENTION TO TASK, TIME ON TASK, ARRANGE FREQUENT CHECK-INS WITH TEACHER OR

- COUNSELOR FOR REINFORCEMENT
- PREFERENTIAL SEATING
- ATTENTIONAL CUEING: KEY VOCABULARY WORDS FIRST TO PRIME LISTENING, ABBREVIATED ORAL INSTRUCTIONS
- COMBINE VISUAL AND AUDITORY : DEMONSTRATIONS, EXAMPLES, PRACTICE WALK-THROUGHS, FLOW CHARTS, OVERHEAD PROJECTOR, ENCOURAGE VISUALIZATIONS
- INCREASED TEACHER AVAILABILITY: TUTORING, BUDDY SYSTEM, NCR NOTETAKING BY BUDDY, TAPE RECORDED BOOKS, LECTURES.

If the problem is he's disorganized, some of these suggestions will help take off the blindfold.

PROBLEM: DISORGANIZED

NEEDS:
- PROVIDE STRUCTURE, REMINDERS, CALENDARS, CHECKLISTS
- TEACH ORGANIZATION, STUDY SKILLS, TIME MANAGEMENT
- REWARD, REINFORCE SUCCESSIVE APPROXIMATIONS TO GOOD ORGANIZATION
- REPEATED AND SIMPLIFIED INSTRUCTIONS FOR ASSIGNMENTS
- ADJUST CLASS SCHEDULE
- HAVE HIM ESTIMATE TIME REQUIRED TO REINFORCE CLOSE APPROXIMATION

If the problem is he's impulsive, the following ideas will bring some needed relief. Then not only does the blindfold come off, but the world view gets rosier.

PROBLEM: IMPULSIVE

NEEDS:
- COGNITIVE BEHAVIOR TRAINING IN SYSTEMATIC, REFLECTIVE PROBLEM SOLVING
- CONTROLLED ENVIRONMENT THAT LIMITS CHOICES
- REINFORCEMENT FOR USE OF MATURE PROBLEM SOLVING
- REWARD MAKING WELL-THOUGHT-OUT DECISIONS THAT PREVIOUSLY HE MIGHT HAVE DONE HASTILY
- PSYCHOTHERAPY FOR THE HURT, SADNESS, AND NEGATIVE AFFECT THAT INTENSIFIES THE POOR IMPULSE CONTROL AND DRIVENNESS
- HELP HIM SET SHORT TERM GOALS: ONE DAY AT A TIME

If the problem is he is overwhelmed, he stays in trouble with parents and teachers constantly. When I'd send Ty to clean his room on Saturday, I'd say, "You can't go outside like Wynn until your part of your room is clean." An hour later I'd find him sitting on his bed staring ahead or playing with a toy. With my continuing further repeat listing of the bad things that were going to continue to happen if the room wasn't cleaned, his dawdling behavior continued, of course. The light went on, as it should have gone on much sooner, because by then I was already teaching *Pennington Positive Parenting*. I realized that I needed to help him cut the job down into bite-sized pieces, reinforce with praise often, and offer him the reward at the end, rather than to threaten the lack of play time that was facing him.

My tactic changed to "Ty, there's several different jobs here. We've got to pick up toys and put them in the toy box. We've got to put dirty clothes in the hamper. Then we've got to put away your clean clothes, make the bed, and sweep the floor. That's all. Let's make a chart with these on them. What do you want to do first? Pick up toys? Okay, I'll get you started. Great! Come and get me when you've finished and we'll put a check on the chart. In no time you'll be outside playing." Each task was quickly checked off with much praise for his hard work. He was outside in less than an hour after what had been an all-day chore.

If the problem is he's overwhelmed, then he may just as well have his hands tied because nothing gets done and no sense of accomplishment can manifest. But if some of the following ideas are tried, not only do the hands become untied, but it's as though he's been given a pair of scissors to cut things down to size. I untie the volunteer's hands and give him or her scissors.

PROBLEM: OVERWHELMED

NEEDS:
- REINFORCE GETTING STARTED
- PROVIDE SEGMENTED TASKS
- TEACH CHUNKING
- REWARD BREAKING GLOBAL TASKS INTO MANAGEABLE PIECES
- GIVE DIRECTIONS ONE AT A TIME
- REWARD PERSEVERANCE
- REWARD CORRECT COMPLETION OF WORK SEGMENTS
- MODIFY TEST DELIVERY: VERBAL, TAPED
- UNTIMED TESTS IN ISOLATION
- HELP WITH TEST ANXIETY
- TAILORED HOMEWORK ASSIGNMENTS
- COMPUTER-AID: TALK INTO TAPE RECORDER, LATER TRANSCRIBE WRITTEN WORK

I've seen it happen so often. ADHD kids get so many negatives that they get rather emotionally guarded. It's hard to get beyond the facade to know how they really feel. Its as though they're all bound up in the chest and one can't get beyond the armor the child has built up defensively over the years. It requires real skill – an acceptance of where that child is emotionally and the ability to really listen to his feelings - to be able to truly be there for him or her. But if such skills are honed and practiced, the armor melts and the child or teen is able to experience some good feelings, too, for a change. I give my volunteer a small clown after I remove the binding from his chest.

PROBLEM: EMOTIONALLY GUARDED

NEEDS:
- ACCEPT HIM WHERE HE IS
- USE LISTENING SKILLS FOR FEELINGS UNDERNEATH
- ALLOW FACE SAVING
- AVOID STIGMATIZED "HELP"

- USE NON-CRITICAL I-MESSAGES
- PROVIDE SUPPORT GROUP
- USE ENCOURAGEMENT

Over years and months of negative feedback from parents and teachers, ADHD kids start to develop low self esteem. It's as though his legs are tied together because he can't emotionally stand on his own two feet. He doesn't trust his own abilities, so he won't try tasks – sometimes even fun things – that might offer a challenge. Such depreciation of his own abilities can become a paralyzing self-fulfilling prophecy. By trying these interventions, you help unbind his legs so he can start to think about standing on his own two feet. Use praise that is USHIC. Don't muddy the waters with a negative at the end of your praise such as, "You did a good job on that. But next time try even harder."

PROBLEM: LOW SELF ESTEEM
NEEDS:
- BUILD SUCCESS INTO HIS LIFE
- STRENGTH BOMBARDMENT: HAVE HIM LIST ONE POSITIVE THING ABOUT HIMSELF DAILY
- APPRECIATION EXERCISES: EACH FAMILY MEMBER TELS THE OTHER, "WHAT I APPRECIATE ABOUT YOU IS....."
- POSITIVE PARENTING
- USE **USHIC** PRAISE: UNCONTAMINATED, SPECIFIC, HONEST, IMMEDIATE, CONSISTENT
- PRAISE THE EFFORT NOT, "YOU'RE SO SMART."
- POSITIVE TEACHING
- PARENTS AND TEACHERS MUST REFRAME THEIR VIEW OF HIM:
- HE'S NOT UNCOOPERATIVE; HE HAS A BIOCHEMICAL DEFICIT

If his self concept remains low for weeks, months, years, this low mood can develop into depression. The inability to stand up emotionally becomes chronic and debilitating because fatigue, indecision, sadness, and other factors pull the emotional floor out from under the child. By using the following interventions, the parent is helping the ADHD child to stand up and to re-enter the mainstream of life with more energy and vigor.

PROBLEM: DEPRESSED

NEEDS:
- THOROUGH RULE-OUT ASSESSMENT
- THOROUGH ASSESSMENT OF SEQUELAE (WHICH CAME FIRST, THE CHICKEN OR THE EGG?)
- PSYCHOTHERAPY: FAMILY, GROUP, INDIVIDUAL
- IMPROVE SCHOOL FUNCTIONING
- STIMULANT MEDICATION MAY BE CONTRAINDICATED
- MAY NEED TO HAVE LESS DEMANDING SCHEDULE
- REGULAR SUNLIGHT AND EXERCISE
- OMEGA 3 FISH OIL

If the problem is his social skills are poor - and they often are with ADHD, it's as though his arms are bound by his side. By doing the following, you will allow him the courage to start to reach out and touch others and experience a little community and love. I remove the binding holding my volunteer's arms against his chest allowing him to receive the miniature heart I hold out to him symbolizing love.

PROBLEM: POOR SOCIAL SKILLS

NEEDS:
- TEACH SOCIAL SKILLS: LISTENING SKILLS & COMPLIMENTS AMONG OTHERS
- ESTABLISH PEER HELPERS
- DE-STIGMATIZE HELP
- USE COOPERATIVE LEARNING, CLUSTERED SEATING
- GROUP CONTINGENCIES CAN IMPROVE PEER STATUS
- TRY SOCIOMETRIC GROUPING WITH CLASS STARS
- ARRANGE BIG SISTERS, BIG BROTHERS

When chronic illness, a physical or mental disability, alcoholism, or other conditions are present, our families of ADHD kids get temporarily or permanently off balance or out of kilter. It's as though the family system is a mobile like those you place over a baby's crib. If one part of the system is set in motion, the whole rest of the system reacts to the motion. In my family, my chronic severe allergies and asthma, my husband's alcoholism, and Ty's ADHD all played their part in setting our family into dysfunctional patterns. One parent starts to over-function, the other becomes more emotionally distant, one child grows wings and a halo, and the other child gets more than his fair share of negative attention. This was the type of family I grew up in and darned if I didn't grow up and recreate it with my own family. It is very hard to step back and understand these set family roles. It is even more difficult to recognize your part in it and change it.

Even though I'm still working through the pain of seeing my brother so abused emotionally and physically by our very frustrated father, I had to get healthier in my family interactions as a grown up. I decided my husband did not have the right to conclude that he was not cut out to work, drink all night, and sleep all day. I decided that I could delegate even more of the load of running the family household rather than feeling so overburdened. I realized Ty wasn't always to blame for everything that went wrong in our family. I was able eventually to remove more binding from Ty's legs, my own, and Wynn's too, so that we no longer were stuck in the dysfunctional roles we'd almost become cemented into.

We could break out of those bonds and walk our own path in our own hand-made shoes. It is here that I help the volunteer out of his chair, hand him a pair of running shoes. In my family, we could now even take off running without the tight grip our old family roles had had upon us. Try these ideas if you want to break the too tight dysfunctional role boundaries, so you and your family are able to not only stand up but take off running, each in his own special individual race. Sometimes you have to get some help outside the family system to be able to change it to healthier ways to be. You must get treatment for the chronic illnesses, handicaps, or addictions that keep things off kilter in your family.

PROBLEM: FAMILY DYSFUNCTION
NEEDS:
- TEACH/LEARN POSITIVE PARENTING SKILLS
- PARENT SUPPORT GROUPS
- TEACH/LEARN STRESS MANAGEMENT SKILLS
- FAMILY THERAPY
- MARITAL THERAPY
- TWELVE STEP GROUPS

From what we know about successful ADHD adults, they have been able to receive much of the good stuff that removed or reduced many of the bindings I've described. They got help from somewhere to take off the ear plugs, remove the blinders, untie the hands, unbind the feelings, help them reach out to others, stand on their own two feet, and walk their own unique path, rather than being forced into prescribed roles.

SUCCESSFUL ADHD ADULTS...
- TAKE CONTROL OF THEIR LIVES
- MAKE CONSCIOUS DECISIONS
- FIND AND ENHANCE STRENGTHS
- ADAPTABLE: PERSISTENT, CREATE GOODNESS OF FIT
- LEARN CREATIVELY, CREATE AND USE SUPPORT SYSTEMS
- DESIRE FOR ACHIEVEMENT
- GOAL SETTING: IDENTIFY REALISTIC AMBITIONS, FOCUS ON ACTIVITIES THAT ARE IMPORTANT, GOAL ACHIEVEMENT SNOWBALLS
- REFRAMING SYMPTOMS POSITIVELY: RECOGNIZE, ACCEPT, UNDERSTAND, ACT

What Research Shows About Effectiveness of Various Treatments of ADHD

Parent Training Compares Well To Medication

I wrote a paper years ago called, "*Parent Behavior Management Training as an Adjunct or Alternative to Methyphenidate (Ritalin) in Treatment for Attention Deficit Disorder*" I first presented these data in an invited presentation to the Georgia Association of School Psychologists (GASP) in 1984 about my study of the effectiveness of parent training compared to stimulant medication. I reported the same data to more of my colleagues the next year in an invited presentation to the Georgia Council for Exceptional Children about my parent workshop I had developed and been using for years. I had first developed the parent training course for use with severely mentally handicapped youngsters and adults, severely brain damaged folks, and autistic people. I had great success with this population by training parents and other care takers. Later I had used *Pennington Positive Parenting* with milder learning disabled youngsters, discipline problem kids, and behaviorally disordered kids along with the many children I would see as a school psychologist in the public school back then who had what later became known as ADHD.

It was only at one of Atlanta's premier hospitals where I was the director of a pediatric psychology program, that I was able to specifically and exclusively target an ADHD population in my *Pennington Positive Parenting* workshop. As the director of the ground-breaking Northside Hospital's Child Development Institute I was able to train two of my staff to teach the course at night along with me so that we could have the course running continuously. I cited in that paper my concern from the research at that time in the ADHD field about the long term outcome showing ADHD patients more at risk in adulthood than normal peers for frequent job change, marital discord, car accidents, delinquency, school and job failure, and antisocial problems. The poor long term outcome for many ADHD adults remains in poor driving records, chronic employment and relationship issues according to the most recent research by Barkley and colleagues' reported at CHADD in 2006. I was hoping that my parent training could start to make a difference in these kids' lives. I think it did for the children I treated.

My subjects for this study were mostly referred to my hospital program by pediatricians. Each of the children were given a full psychological evaluation, which found them to be exhibiting the signs and symptoms of ADHD. Ages of the children were 3 to 13 with at least average IQ as measured by the Wechsler Scale; most were boys in two-parent, middle class homes. No control group without treatment was used because we were a clinical facility and could not discourage parents from pursuing any appropriate treatment immediately for their children.

The project included thirty-six children whose parents completed the forms necessary to be part of the study - roughly half the parents who actually attended. (And we parents complain about our kids not getting homework done!) The course lasted six weeks, meeting one evening a week for two hours. In more than half the families only the mother attended even though evening hours were offered purposively to encourage father participation. Parents were encouraged to choose only one behavior to target in the group. The following behaviors were addressed by various parents: bed wetting, remaining seated at table, impulse control, climbing on furniture, sibling quarrels, non compliance, dressing on time, home chores, homework completion, classroom disruptive behavior, classwork completion, verbal aggression, father-son relationship, fire setting, finicky eating, temper outbursts, negative self concept, and restaurant behavior.

Pre-treatment and post-treatment data were gathered in the form of the Stress/Burnout Form for parents, designed by the author and normed on colleagues in the mental health center inside the general hospital where my pediatric psychology program was housed. Also the Conners' Parent Questionnaire was completed and the Burks' Behavior Rating Scales were completed about the children. On the Burks' the parents rated 118 behaviors on a five-point scale ranging from "not noticed" at a 1 to "noticed to a large degree" marked as 5. The behaviors are sorted into eighteen clusters and scored in the "not significant," "significant," to "very significant" range.

Before and after scores on the Stress/Burnout Form for parents showed considerable improvement in coping skills for the mothers. No change was noted for the dads in their stress responses. So few Conners' forms were returned at the end of the course, no true comparisons could be made.

It was in the Burks' that we saw so much improvement in all the eighteen behavior clusters measured on this instrument. Parents completed a four page form which my staff and I scored onto a one-page summary score sheet. First let's look at how all the kids looked on the Burks' scale before the *Pennington Positive Parenting* group. There were eight behavioral clusters that were scoring into the significant range at the beginning of the course. These were excessive self blame, poor ego strength (a self esteem measure), poor academics, poor attention, poor impulse control, poor anger control, excessive aggressiveness, and excessive resistance. See Table 1.

TABLE 1: *BEFORE* INTERVENTION GROUP PARENT TRAINING

Behavioral Clusters (Note scales to right)--->	Score	Not Significant |--------------->	Significant <--------------->	Very Significant <---------------|
EXCESSIVE SELF BLAME	10.98		x	
EXCESSIVE ANXIETY	8.70	x		
EXCESSIVE WITHDRAWAL	8.78	x		
EXCESSIVE DEPENDENCY	11.82	x		
POOR EGO STRENGTH	15.90		x	
POOR PHYSICAL STENGTH	6.71	x		
POOR COORDINATION	9.29	x		
POOR INTELLECTUALITY	12.90	x		
POOR ACADEMICS	11.47		x	
POOR ATTENTION	15.34		x	
POOR IMPULSE CONTROL	14.79		x	
POOR REALTIY CONTACT	12.47	x		
POOR SENSE OF IDENTITY	7.82	x		
EXCESSIVE SUFFERING	13.43	x		
POOR ANGER CONTROL	13.70		x	
EXCESSIVE SENSE OF PERSECUTION	9.98	x		
EXCESSIVE AGGRESSIVENESS	14.66		x	
EXCESSIVE RESISTANCE	13.02		x	
POOR SOCIAL CONFORMITY	15.86	x		

Here are the scores the thirty-six children earned after the parents attended six weeks of parent training. Notice the movement back toward the left into the non-significant range for all scores even though parents were only targeting one or two behaviors. The only scores that remained in the significant range were poor attention, poor impulse control, poor anger control, and excessive resistance, and each of these placed only barely into the significant range. Parents were able to bring even these resistant problems down to a manageable level. See Table 2:

Table 2: *AFTER* INTERVENTION GROUP PARENT TRAINING

Behavioral Clusters (Note scales to right)--->	Score	Not Significant |---------------->	Significant <---------------->	Very Significant <----------------|
EXCESSIVE SELF BLAME	8.10	0		
EXCESSIVE ANXIETY	8.04	0		
EXCESSIVE WITHDRAWAL	8.24	0		
EXCESSIVE DEPENDENCY	10.01	0		
POOR EGO STRENGTH	12.22	0		
POOR PHYSICAL STENGTH	6.53	0		
POOR COORDINATION	8.65	0		
POOR INTELLECTUALITY	11.32	0		
POOR ACADEMICS	8.98	0		
POOR ATTENTION	12.14		0	
POOR IMPULSE CONTROL	11.79		0	
POOR REALTIY CONTACT	10.99	0		
POOR SENSE OF IDENTITY	6.83	0		
EXCESSIVE SUFFERING	11.07	0		
POOR ANGER CONTROL	11.08		0	
EXCESSIVE SENSE OF PERSECUTION	7.97	0		
EXCESSIVE AGGRESSIVENESS	10.33	0		
EXCESSIVE RESISTANCE	11.10		0	
POOR SOCIAL CONFORMITY	13.35	0		

It turned out that the parents of three children chose to put the subjects on medication in the middle of the *Pennington Positive Parenting* workshop. We really could not attribute their improvement to the parent training, so those three kids were factored out of the data on the next chart and only the thirty-three who did not have another intervention introduced mid-treatment remained. This is how those kids looked before the parents started the training. Once again the same eight clusters scored in the significant range before treatment, so this group looked very similar to the full group. See Table 3

TABLE 3: *BEFORE* GROUP *PENNINGTON POSITIVE PARENT* TRAINING
(no medication introduced simultaneously)

Behavioral Clusters (Note scales to right)--->	Score	Not Significant |--------------->	Significant <--------------->	Very Significant <---------------|
EXCESSIVE SELF BLAME	10.68		x	
EXCESSIVE ANXIETY	8.61	x		
EXCESSIVE WITHDRAWAL	8.99	x		
EXCESSIVE DEPENDENCY	11.93	x		
POOR EGO STRENGTH	16.12		x	
POOR PHYSICAL STENGTH	6.83	x		
POOR COORDINATION	9.20	x		
POOR INTELLECTUALITY	13.08	x		
POOR ACADEMICS	11.50		x	
POOR ATTENTION	15.38		x	
POOR IMPULSE CONTROL	14.86		x	
POOR REALTIY CONTACT	12.43	x		
POOR SENSE OF IDENTITY	7.87	x		
EXCESSIVE SUFFERING	13.29	x		
POOR ANGER CONTROL	15.50		x	
EXCESSIVE SENSE OF PERSECUTION	9.82	x		
EXCESSIVE AGGRESSIVENESS	14.88		x	
EXCESSIVE RESISTANCE	13.04		x	
POOR SOCIAL CONFORMITY	16.12	x		

Take a look at how these kids who only had the workshop during the six weeks without medication contaminating the data fared after their parents were taught *Pennington Positive Parenting* techniques. At the end of six weeks, almost all clusters had moved toward the left - the non-significant range. There was improvement toward the "not noticed at all" column in these behaviors: self blame, dependency, coordination, intellectuality, academics, reality contact, sense of identity, suffering (a depression index), sense of persecution, aggressiveness, and social conformity. Only four clusters remained in the significant range and just barely. They were the same ones as in the full group: poor attention, poor impulse control, poor anger control, and excessive resistance. Excessive self blame, poor ego strength, poor academics, and excessive aggressiveness had disappeared from the significant range.

Now that these ADHD's were basking in the positive environment created by their newly diligent parents, they no longer got upset if things didn't turn out perfectly. Their view of themselves became one of competence; their academics also improved even though not all parents were targeting homework or school related behaviors. No longer were these kids aggressive toward peers and siblings. So it really was the parent training alone that made such huge differences, bringing the kids' behavior to within manageable limits. Wow! See Table 4.

TABLE 4: *AFTER* GROUP *PENNINGTON POSITIVE PARENT* TRAINING

(no medication introduced simultaneously)

Behavioral Clusters (Note scales to right)--->	Score	Not Significant |---------------->	Significant <---------------->	Very Significant <----------------|
EXCESSIVE SELF BLAME	8.04	0		
EXCESSIVE ANXIETY	8.07	0		
EXCESSIVE WITHDRAWAL	8.33	0		
EXCESSIVE DEPENDENCY	10.27	0		
POOR EGO STRENGTH	12.37	0		
POOR PHYSICAL STENGTH	6.67	0		
POOR COORDINATION	8.68	0		
POOR INTELLECTUALITY	11.50	0		
POOR ACADEMICS	9.23	0		
POOR ATTENTION	12.59		0	
POOR IMPULSE CONTROL	12.09		0	
POOR REALTIY CONTACT	11.13	0		
POOR SENSE OF IDENTITY	6.94	0		
EXCESSIVE SUFFERING	11.24	0		
POOR ANGER CONTROL	11.38		0	
EXCESSIVE SENSE OF PERSECUTION	8.00	0		
EXCESSIVE AGGRESSIVENESS	10.53	0		
EXCESSIVE RESISTANCE	11.32		0	
POOR SOCIAL CONFORMITY	13.62	0		

I was able to obtain Burks' data on eleven of these same thirty-six children who went on medication either before or after the *Pennington Positive Parenting* workshop. These data are eye opening when one compares them to the success of parent training. In these eleven cases there were six clusters in the significant range and one, poor attention, that measured a bit into the very significant range before medication. See Table 5

TABLE 5: MEDICATION ALONE - PRE-INTERVENTION

Behavioral Clusters (Note scales to right)--->	Score	Not Significant |--------------->	Significant <--------------->	Very Significant <---------------|
EXCESSIVE SELF BLAME	11.27		X	
EXCESSIVE ANXIETY	9.05	X		
EXCESSIVE WITHDRAWAL	9.05	X		
EXCESSIVE DEPENDENCY	12.23	X		
POOR EGO STRENGTH	14.87		X	
POOR PHYSICAL STENGTH	7.18	X		
POOR COORDINATION	9.37	X		
POOR INTELLECTUALITY	13.55	X		
POOR ACADEMICS	7.91	X		
POOR ATTENTION	18.82			X
POOR IMPULSE CONTROL	16.96		X	
POOR REALTIY CONTACT	12.50	X		
POOR SENSE OF IDENTITY	7.00	X		
EXCESSIVE SUFFERING	13.77	X		
POOR ANGER CONTROL	14.86		X	
EXCESSIVE SENSE OF PERSECUTION	8.18	X		
EXCESSIVE AGGRESSIVENESS	12.52		X	
EXCESSIVE RESISTANCE	14.77		X	
POOR SOCIAL CONFORMITY	17.85		X	

Most experts and parents who have tried it agree that stimulant medication can be very effective. I agree, too. Here are the Burks' profiles of the eleven children who tried medication either before or after the six weeks of parent training. Attention problems moved from the very significant range to the significant, but not quite as far to the good as parent training moved this cluster. Note that poor academics was not a problem before medication but became significant after medication. I have no explanation for this change. The other significant problems remaining after medication had moved back toward the norm at about the same level as with the parent training group. Overall results of parent training were the same or slightly, but not significantly, better than medication. See Table 6 on the following page.

TABLE 6: MEDICATION ALONE – POST-INTERVENTION

Behavioral Clusters (Note scales to right)--->	Score	Not Significant |------------------>	Significant <------------------>	Very Significant <------------------|
EXCESSIVE SELF BLAME	9.27	0		
EXCESSIVE ANXIETY	8.14	0		
EXCESSIVE WITHDRAWAL	8.73	0		
EXCESSIVE DEPENDENCY	10.64	0		
POOR EGO STRENGTH	12.73	0		
POOR PHYSICAL STENGTH	6.18	0		
POOR COORDINATION	5.86	0		
POOR INTELLECTUALITY	10.05	0		
POOR ACADEMICS	10.83		0	
POOR ATTENTION	13.91		0	
POOR IMPULSE CONTROL	13.32		0	
POOR REALTIY CONTACT	11.18	0		
POOR SENSE OF IDENTITY	7.18	0		
EXCESSIVE SUFFERING	12.41	0		
POOR ANGER CONTROL	11.96		0	
EXCESSIVE SENSE OF PERSECUTION	8.43	0		
EXCESSIVE AGGRESSIVENESS	11.41	0		
EXCESSIVE RESISTANCE	11.41		0	
POOR SOCIAL CONFORMITY	14.53	0		

Nine months to a year later follow up forms were mailed to the participants in the study. None were returned. Thus phone interviews were held, but only the parents of seven children in the study could be contacted who were willing to take the time to answer the 118 questions over the phone. At nine months to a year follow up, it was found that all these children were now on medication. The token economy was being used unevenly without continued support for the parents to keep the behavior change going. The same four behavioral clusters remained in the significant range at about the same level of intensity as at the end of the parent training program. These were : poor attention, poor impulse control, poor anger control, and excessive aggressiveness, but the last one only barely.

It appears that it is hard to maintain gains made in changing family environment without some kind of continued support. It was after these data came in that I instituted monthly parent support groups for alumni of my training course. The reader should be aware that continued vigilance is required to maintain gains made when one is in the thick of making rapid, dramatic improvements in family atmosphere. To ensure such new positive habits are maintained, review work should be done regularly along with attendance to a support group.

It has also been my experience that just reading the book doesn't help parents make the required changes at home unless they are very motivated. Attendance in a *Pennington Positive Parenting* course or diligent use of the *Pennington Positive Parenting* DVD seems necessary.

National Study Shows Behavioral and Medication Treatments Together Produce Best Results

The most thorough study to date of various ADHD treatment outcomes was sponsored by the National Institute of Mental Health reported in 1999. It was called the Multimodal Treatment Study of ADHD Children (MTA for short). It examined at one-year follow up how 579 ADHD kids at six different sites around the country were faring after having been randomly assigned to several groups. Those treated with behavior therapy did slightly better than the other groups including the medication group. Later, a subsequent report in 2004 following the same children for a longer time found the multi-modal group – those who received medication as well as behavior therapy - doing better than other groups.

What We Know About ADHD Kids Grown Up

Howell, Huessy and Hassuk in Vermont back in 1985 did a study of almost 400 ADHD youth, following them for fifteen years. The average age when the subjects were identified by their teachers was seven; twenty- two was the average age when the subjects were tracked down and interviewed. The original identification of the subjects consisted of having teachers complete behavior rating scales on all the children in their classes. The kids who scored significantly into the ADHD range were tagged. No treatment was pursued as part of this study; it was done to find out what would happen if the kids were just left alone without any treatment. On all measures of adult competence, the untreated ADHD young adults were not faring well fifteen years after identification, significantly different from their normal peers, who were also interviewed at follow up. Untreated ADHD adults were significantly less likely to have completed high school, far less likely to have pursued post secondary education, far more likely to have been suspended from school, and far more likely to be employed as a low level laborer. These young people reported far more reading problems in school and many more job changes than peers. They were significantly more likely to consider themselves accident prone, to have been in recent trouble with the police, to have been rejected for military enlistment, been arrested, and reporting regular marijuana use at least once per day. These are pretty abysmal outcomes if somehow you fall through the cracks and don't get the help you deserve.

Sponsored by NIMH, Dr. James Satterfield and his colleagues in California in 1989 reported another of the earlier studies to monitor late adolescent and young adult outcome for ADHD. He monitored 91 young males from about age eight to eighteen. He found that only the kids who got medication as well as several other psychological therapies fared well. The therapies offered the boys were individual therapy, family therapy, group therapy and educational therapy. The youth who exhibited the best late adolescent outcome participated in about three of these therapies at a rate of once per week for about three years. Those treated with medication alone had a extremely high arrest record for felonies by age eighteen. It is unclear whether or not the boys were still being treated with medication at follow up. This was one of the first studies showing that medication alone is not the answer for this chronic condition.

Weiss and Hechtman studied ADHD kids grown up in one of these early studies to look at longitudinal data to examine adult outcome. In their book, <u>Hyperactive Children Grown Up</u>, eighty-one ADHD folks were studied. Most adult subjects reported wishing they had had more individual psychotherapy growing up. Many reported such therapy as empowering and helpful to make them to feel more grown up. Most also cited wishing they had had more individual tutoring and remedial education. Many subjects wished they had had more family counseling. They felt this modality had helped their parents understand them better and interact more constructively with them, Many wished they had had more clarification of the problem of ADHD. Many of these adults reported they had never really understood what was wrong with them and neither had their parents.

An unexpected finding was the degree of negative feeling about having to take medication in childhood. Mostly these issues were related to embarrassment and feeling different without an explanation as to why they were having to take it. A quarter of the adults considered medication to have been harmful. The rest saw the benefits, but still disliked taking it. This study certainly suggests that more thorough explanations of ADHD needs to be given youngsters, and if the decision is made to try stimulant medication, the disorder and the medication should be explained to the youngster so that he feels a part of the decision.

ADHD TREATMENT IN A NUTSHELL

Remember to notice how creative, funny, cheery, spontaneous, bouncy, loving, enthusiastic, resilient, and talented these kids and adults can be. Don't let their wonderful characteristics get lost when you focus on changing undesirable behavior. Cut him some slack from drilling on his spelling every day. He may never be very good at it. But he might be a gifted story teller, carpenter, musician, designer, or comedian. Imagine what a dull world it would be if all the animals had to go to school with the same curriculum. Birds would flunk running, but not be as good at flying if they had to spend all their extra time practicing running. Treasure your child for his own wonderful uniqueness.

Review, Application, and Homework for Chapter 7

1. One of the prerequisites of ADHD symptom presentation is an organ that is _____.

2. An environment that focuses on the _____ is more likely to produce ADHD symptoms.

3. Entrance into _____ makes ADHD symptoms more evident.

4. Several recommended ways to increase the availability of noradrenaline and dopamine are:

   _____

   _____

5. Research is showing that one type of treatment is not the only answer, rather _____ therapy brings the best outcome.

6. Parents should give praise that is _____ to avoid cognitive dissonance.

7. Praise should be clear and _____ to avoid having the person feel even worse after it is given.

8. Parent training has been shown to be a powerful _____ or alternative to medication in some children with ADHD.

9. Continue your behavior change project using behavior modification, chart it and pat yourself on the back for doing it.

answers: I. different II. negative III. school IV. positive environment, omega three fish oil, aerobic exercise, possibly play V. multi modality therapy VI. specific VII. uncontaminated VIII. adjunct

CHAPTER SEVEN

MY PLAN FOR IMPROVEMENT

My plan to assume more of a role of helping, encouraging and teaching in my family is
_____

I will know the plan is working when _____

I plan to do less of these (circle all that apply): discount others' feelings, judging, blaming, lecturing, put downs, feeling guilty, etc._____

I plan to do more these (circle all that apply): encouragement, I-messages, reflective listening, validation of others' feelings, offers to help, USHIC praise, etc._____

The specifics of my plan are:

Monday_____

Tuesday_____

Wednesday_____

Thursday_____

Friday_____

Saturday_____

Sunday_____

Complete this page, photocopy it, and carry it with you daily.

CHAPTER 8

HOW TO LISTEN SO YOUR KIDS WILL TALK

All of us parents want desperately to communicate with our children. We puzzle over why they won't talk to us when we are so all ears and so eager to hear what they have to say. We've already learned how to talk to them so they will be more likely to listen to us by practicing assertive communication in the form of "I-messages". We are learning to refrain from rehashing how angry we are at our kids and get down under the anger iceberg to the hurt and worry when we use assertive communication. We also know that we need to share our real feelings with them in a form of a one-word feeling rather than a long-winded explanation that usually gets back to what's wrong with them. We've been talking to our kids in this respectful manner for a while, realizing that unless we treat them with positive regard, they will not do the same with us. We've not been switching into lecture mode that we so loved to do in the past. Now we're asking often for our kids to repeat back what we say so we know they've really heard us. If we practice such messages of authenticity for a while, we start to notice that our kids are more likely to share with us what's really going on with them.

Write out the above things that you are remembering to do more of:

_____

_____

_____

Now we need to address how well we listen to our kids. If we listen better to our kids, they will be more likely to talk to us. Remember that a big reason they don't listen to us is that we often don't listen to them. Research has found that the biggest barrier to good listening is being male. Belenky, Clinchy, Goldberger, and Tarule in <u>Womens' Ways of Knowing</u> as early as 1986 cited eight peer reviewed journal articles that showed consistent and large differences in men's poor ability to listen compared to women in both public and private domains. Men tend to dominate and interrupt others in conversation much more than women. You men who are reading this, please take note and increase your awareness of this tendency and set about changing it. We all can learn to change. That's what this book is all about.

Dr. Carl Rogers several decades ago wrote and taught about his idea that we all possess the ability to solve our own problems if someone will only hold up an "ear" mirror to us, reflecting back what we say so that we can look further inward. What an affirmation to our kids' intelligence it is to let them know that we believe in their own abilities to solve life's challenges rather than train them to expect us to solve problems for them.

Imagine if your youngster walked into the back door just getting home from school, slammed the door and cried, "I'm so stupid!"

What could you say that would help the child express his feelings more and tell you how he got to that place of feeling so rotten? Here are some typical parental responses. You decide by writing "Yes" or "No" beside each response as to whether you'd feel like talking more it you heard that response from someone. Child says, "I'm so stupid."

Parent's Response	**Would You Want to Talk More?**
You mustn't feel that way.	_____
Stop feeling sorry for yourself!	_____
You don't look like a goof-ball to me.	_____
Oh, just go get your mind off it.	_____
You ought to be thankful for all your learning opportunities.	_____
Don't talk like that.	_____
If I were you, I'd talk to a psychologist.	_____
You're only hurting yourself by feeling that way	_____
You should think about yourself in other ways.	_____
People often think that way even when they're bright like you.	_____
You are such a baby.	_____
You're just tired.	_____
You're just hungry and sleepy.	_____
You'll feel better after a nice vacation.	_____
Why do you feel that way?	_____
Just forget about it.	_____
If I were you, I'd just.......	_____
Why can't you just snap out of it?	_____
It's time you got serious about your studies.	_____
Of course you are. You never study.	_____

If you answered "No" to all the above, you are agreeing with what most people report. When people's feelings are not truly heard, discounted, joked about, lectured, or questioned, they are not willing to share more of themselves for fear of more of the same. If they are told they need to see a psychologist just for feeling stupid, they will hesitate to talk more so you can really know how they feel. If such feelings persist and become chronic, that's another story, but we shouldn't be jumping to such conclusions quickly.

Even when we ask our kids, "Why do you feel that way?" they usually answer, "I don't know." Adults rarely know why we feel things, and kids don't know either. With such a question, we're stuck not moving forward to hear more about the problem or come up with a way to help him think of ways to make it better.

Most of the time until we really practice reflective listening for a while, what we say to our children when they come to us with problems actually shuts them up, closing the door to communication. Our lectures, advice giving, or closed messages mean that kids are less likely to keep talking to us and even less likely to come to us the next time with their heart-felt issues.

Now we're going to improve our abilities to listen so that our children and teens feel heard and respected by us. We choose not to talk when we're trying to listen. We're choosing to listen, truly listen, not be a speaker just waiting for our turn to talk. We've put aside assuming we know what the child is going to say even if we've had this conversation a hundred times. We are now choosing to listen to our kids to learn from them, not to decide whether they are right or wrong. We are going to allow our child to teach us how it feels to be in her emotional shoes. Rather than interrupting and dominating the conversation, we are now showing him we're listening with eye contact, nodding our head, body leaning forward, arms uncrossed and open. We show even more connection to the child or teen by sitting or standing close to the young person.

Such body language conveys ninety percent of our message: that we are there for them with our whole being. We must become aware of our non-verbal language and practice good-listening body language often if we are to become truly good listeners. I had one whole graduate course devoted to effective listening in which we students were video taped and critiqued as to how well we conveyed the message that we were present and truly listening to the speaker. The fact that so much time was devoted to teaching and learning good listening speaks to the fact that it is so important and the fact that it is so seldom practiced in the everyday world. Effective, reflective listening takes a lot of practice to get really good at it.

Here are some more effective responses that carry the message to the child that we are taking time to be truly there for them, accept where they are, and that we really want to understand and help. Such messages imply that we know they are capable of solving the problem if we will only listen and show them we are listening.

Child's Statement	*Reflective Listening Response*
I don't want to ever play with Janie again!	*You're really mad at her.*
You are so mean.	*Sounds like you're angry at me.*
I wish I didn't have to go to school.	*You sound worried about things.*
My brother always gets to do stuff.	*You must be feeling neglected.*
It's not cold. I'm not wearing that jacket.	*You're afraid your jacket is no good.*

Now you try some:

My teacher is so mean. _____

I hate spelling. _____

I'm the only one that has to do chores. _____

Homework is stupid. I'm not doing it. _____

I'm not going to bed. _____

I'm so stupid. _____

These new rules are stupid. _____

You write some statements that your child might say and a good response to keep them talking.

_____

_____

_____

_____

_____

_____

_____

_____

This type of reflective listening that I'm advocating requires taking time to listen – really listen – to the feelings behind and beneath the words. It can be called listening with a third ear. That ear being attuned to a more human, emotional reality that needs warmth, comfort, and solace. This type of listening means you just paraphrase back what you're hearing. Not really a parroting, but a reflection that shows the speaker he's being heard.

Rather than parroting back, "Polly wants a cracker," you'd be more likely to reflect, "You're hungry and want something to eat. "

Notice that if you practice this better listening with people, after a reflective listening response, they are likely to tell you more. Another such reflective response brings more information and more sharing. After several more, often garnered with a statement as, "Tell me more about that," you start to get to the bottom of the problem. Then you might even could add the humorous response (You don't look like a goof-ball to me.) or the generalizing response (Other people feel that way too, even when they're bright like you.) that lets the person know he is not the only one ever to have those feelings.

Next it's time to try brainstorming. Finally you can ask a question. You ask the youngster, "What do you think you need to do differently next time?"

If he shrugs an "I don't know," encourage him to venture an idea no matter how crazy it might seem. You offer a nutty idea, too, to start the ball rolling. Before you know it, you both are adding ideas to consider. Do not criticize any idea no matter how far fetched it may be.

After several ideas are offered, you and the youth decide together which one might work best. A plan is made, and you agree to talk again in about a week to see how things are going.

Lets' go back to the first example when your child says, "I'm so stupid." You might reply, "Sounds as though you're feeling down on yourself."

Child: "Yeah, that's the truth!"

Parent: "So, you really had a bad day today and you're feeling dumb."

Child: "The kids laughed at me when I gave the wrong answer in social studies."

Parent: "The kids gave you a hard time when you gave a wrong answer."

Child: "Yeah, I guess I wasn't paying attention, and I didn't read the chapter very well last night."

Parent: "You're thinking you might not be putting enough time into reading the chapters. Your mind might be wandering off."

Child: "Yeah, when I was doing my homework, I was listening to the other kids playing outside the window and getting distracted."

Parent: "Sounds like you may have already figured out what you need to do to change things."

Child: "I think I need to close my window so I don't hear them playing."

Parent: "Why don't you try that for a while, and let's talk next week and see how it goes."

More than twenty years ago I ran a group for learning disabled kids, some of whom had what is now called ADHD. I volunteered to facilitate the group sponsored by the Georgia Association for Children with Learning Disabilities. Remember that most ADHD kids have another learning disability (LD) in addition to their ADHD. In that group of LD and ADHD kids, I asked the children to write any question they wanted me to answer and turn it in anonymously. It was in that group that I could really put my reflective listening skills to good use to try to hear the real question and the real feelings underneath the question. When you listen to the feelings underneath the words, you might say you are listening with a third ear.

Here are some of the questions they asked of me and my third-ear responses back to the group so they were able to feel heard before I answered the questions:

LD child's question: *"Do lots of people have laening (sic) disabelty (sic)?"* (Note there were also several letter reversals in each question.)

Reflective answer: "You're maybe feeling that you're different. You maybe need to hear that you're not alone – and you're not. You probably want to be able to talk to other kids who have similar problems in a safe place so that you can know you'll be okay."

(Notice I did not correct the spelling. That would have deflated and defeated the child, and shut him up quickly.)

LD child's question: *"Why do I sometimes have a hard time on the computer? Why do I have to go to anthore (sic) class?"*

Reflective answer: "You're wondering why things are so hard for you. You're wondering why you are in a special class. You may be feeling not very bright when you struggle so. You'd like some help understanding your learning style. You'd like a good explanation you can understand of your need for special help so it can be useful and productive for you. The answer starts by your asking this very good, important question."

LD child's question: "*Why did I get a (sic) LD problem?*"

Reflective answer: "You may be wondering if all this is your fault. You may be wondering if you did something bad and you're being punished for it. You need someone to explain the cause of your learning disability in words you can understand."

LD Child's question: "*What does learing (sic) disobelty(sic) mean?*"

Reflective answer: "You're wondering what the term "learning disability" means. Sometimes kids wonder if this means they're retarded. You need an explanation in words you can understand that will convince you that your are not dumb, not mean, and that your condition can be treated. By the way, they all can, and yours is no exception. There are plenty of very successful people who have learning disabilities and ADHD."

LD child's question: "*Why am I here?*"

Reflective response: "You may be wondering why you are on this earth. You're wondering if you really have to face your learning and attention problems. Sounds as if you are asking for an explanation of what is different about you. Without such an explanation you may refuse to participate in treatment or discussion of your issues. Without people treating you with respect and dignity, you question what the benefit of any discussion could be."

LD child's question: "*Why do some people think you are a nerd?*"

Reflective listening response: "You're wondering why other kids don't seem to like you sometimes. You may be wondering why you are so different. You may have questions about your social difficulties and wonder if there is a way to get better at dealing with other kids. You may be wondering if this isolation you could be feeling will get worse. You probably are asking if there is any training that could help you with this and improve you're self esteem. There are may ways to help kids with social skills and self esteem."

LD child's brother's question: "*What are the courses that teachers have to take to teach in schools with L.D. Kids?*"

Reflective listening response: "You may be wondering if, with special help, your sibling will be okay. You could be wondering if you will ever get the skills and patience you need to live with him or her. As a sibling of a kid with chronic problem, just like other siblings of other kids with other chronic problems, you're asking for hope that he will be okay, that his teachers know what they're doing. You may be asking for more help in understanding your brother and your self."

LD child's question: "*Why is (sic) hard to read some time why me and redding (sic) why me?*"

Reflective listening response: "You're wondering why things come so hard for you, especially reading. You might be struggling with what's called a grief process as we come to terms with the fact that we do have some challenges in life and they aren't easy. You may be looking for reassurance that you can cope with your disability so you don't become defined just by your deficits and not your strengths."

LD child's question: *"Why do they start? Do I have a problem? Why?"*

Reflective listening response: "You're wondering what caused this problem. Was it something you did. You're questioning how much you may be affected. You're wondering out of all the people in the world the cosmos had to choose you to give this disorder to. You probably are needing some hope that it is not as bad as you might imagine."

LD child's question: *"whhy (sic) dus (sic) moms (sic) gite (sic) to Be (sic) mehy (sic) ?"*

Reflective listening response: You're wondering why your mom seems so mean to you. You wonder why your parents get so angry at you often. It's hard for you to see the frustration, worry, and guilt underneath the anger they may be feeling when they blow up at you. You're tired of being yelled at for what you see is no reason. You really would like to see your parents get help with their parenting skills so that you and they don't feel so frustrated, hopeless and helpless much of the time. There is help for your family. It's just that someone needs to have the courage to admit the need and seek the help. You've started that process right now with your question."

Homework and Application of Chapter 8

1. Good listening requires an _____ heart and a _____ attitude.

2. Good listening requires that you not just wait for you chance to _____.

3. Good listening is shown by body language such as

   _____

   _____.

4. An example of a _____ response is, "You've been goofing off, so of course your grades are bad."

5. Underneath our anger iceberg is usually _____, _____, or _____.

6. Reflective listening assumes the child _____.

7. Reflective listening is often followed by _____.

8. Brainstorming does _____ involve critical or judgmental remarks.

9. Effective, reflective listen implies that the listener respect the speaker enough to allow the speaker to _____ his own problems.

10. Continue your behavior change project, chart it and reward yourself.

answers: I. open, non-judgmental II. speak. III. leaning forward, eye contact, nodding, arms not crossed. IV. closed or "you," V. hurt and fear or worry VI. can VII. brainstorming VIII. not IX. solve the problem.

193

CHAPTER EIGHT

MY PLAN FOR IMPROVEMENT

My plan to show my family more positive regard and mutual respect is

_____

_____

_____

The way I will know it's better is _____

I will do these things less (circle all that apply) : threatening, nagging, yelling, punishing, shaming, interrupting, lecturing, etc _____

I will do more of these (circle all that apply): reflective listening, encouraging, improving my consistency, brainstorming, doing loving deeds, playing with my family, assertive communication, USHIC praise, etc_____

Specifics of my plan:

Monday_____

Tuesday_____

Wednesday_____

Thursday_____

Friday_____

Saturday_____

Sunday_____

Complete this plan, photocopy it, and carry it with you daily

CHAPTER 9

MANAGE YOUR STRESS BEFORE IT MANAGES YOU

Research by Burt, Cohen, and Bjorck back in 1988 found that cohesive, organized and expressive families were more likely to have well-functioning adolescents than families that were conflict-ridden and controlling. This book has been focused on helping parents design and build cohesive families who are organized and able to express themselves in a positive manner. Such a task is much harder when you're stressed. My most stressful period was when I became a single mother with two toddlers. It followed a violent two-week period when my husband, who was the children's father, stole the rent money and began continually threatening me with a gun. The terror ended only when he abandoned us and fled to another state, leaving the children and me with no money, no food, and facing eviction. I had to work full-time at the only job for which I was qualified at the time: a waitress. I was unable to collect the meager child support I had requested and had been awarded. I was also busy completing my undergraduate degree full time. I was constantly tired and frazzled - not the best mother. The fact that one of my kids, Ty, was a real **HANDFUL** added to the load. I was stressed to the max.

I remember one day I was so stressed out, I forgot Ty and left him at a service station. We were a half mile away before I noticed how quiet it was in the car. Ty wasn't there! I zoomed back to find him sitting on a high stool with a candy bar and a Coke the kind station owner had bought him. Not my shining hour. I hope he's forgiven me by now. I think he has. I know I've worked hard at forgiving myself and forgiving my ex-husband for abandoning us. His DNA helped create two wonderful children who became dynamite adults. What a gift he gave us when he left so that my sons didn't have to witness the toxic effects of his slow decline into further addiction and alcoholism.

I've chosen to view that long-ago time in my life as a learning time. I learned so much from that man. I'm grateful for each experience I endured with him. May he walk in peace as much as I and my sons do right now. At this writing he is gravely ill from the aftermath of his many excesses. *[Ed. note: he passed away as this was going to press.]*

We could have been one of the families Green studied in 1989 when he found ADHD symptoms amplified by an under-organized and chaotic family structure. It's hard to be organized when you're terrified for your life and desperate to find the money to feed and house your children. Konstanyareas and Homatidis in 1989 found us mothers reporting greater stress in response to behavioral difficulties in our kids than dads.

I've suspected for a long time that we parents of ADHD kids are more stressed than other adults and that we might have fewer coping resources. When I was working on my doctorate in psychology, I was able to do some research under the auspices of Georgia State University. My subjects were thirty-nine parents of ADHD children who were willing to complete a questionnaire called Coping Resources Inventory for Stress.

Thousands of people in many different cultures and groups have been studied with this instrument in several continents. No particular group has ever stood out as being any different from the norm for other adults in their ability to cope with stress. Even spouse abusers, famous for their tendency to blame stress and their victims for their behavior, did not differ significantly from the typical adult. Yet I was not particularly shocked to find that we parents of ADHD kids are significantly poorer in our ability to cope with stress. My colleagues at school were surprised. Finding a group so radically different from the adult norms had never happened before.

Twenty-three mothers and sixteen fathers were a part of my study. The children ranged in age from four to fifteen. My working definition of stress for this study was an inequality between perceived demands and perceived resources for dealing with those demands. Notice that its not the outside world that causes our stress, but what we tell ourselves about our ability to handle it.

Besides poorer overall coping resources, parents of ADHD kids displayed significant differences from the normal population in five sub scales and two composite sub scales. We parents report a lower level of perceived acceptance - of ourselves and others. We also report less social support. That is, we don't see family and friends as forthcoming to act as buffers against stressful life events. I know that I didn't have nearby family to call on for childcare and other support during my most stressful times.

It seems that parents of ADHD children are less likely to be in families that communicate well with each other and exhibit love and affection. Such families do not handle conflict well either. It's hard to communicate love and affection when the grocery and rent money is spent every week on booze and pot. A loaded gun is not a recommended conflict resolution tool, either.

I also found that parents of ADHD's were more likely to report perceived stress from perception of lack of financial freedom. We moved thirteen times the year before I defied my husband's orders and insisted I would find a job. We parents of ADHD kids are also less aware of our own personal stress and tension build-up, so that before we know it, we're stressed to the max and don't know how we got there. Lack of tension control was the most dramatic finding. It seems that we parents of ADHD's possess less ability to lower our arousal levels through relaxation and thought control. We are less likely than other adults to identify and change our thinking that produces even more stress. We tend to hold onto dysfunctional beliefs such as, "I can't be happy if others disapprove of me." or, "I have to be good at all things to be worthwhile." or, "The world should meet my wishes at all times."

This information is useful to design further treatment alternatives to complement the traditional treatments of ADHD: medication, psycho educational training of the parents, and cognitive behavioral therapy. We parents must be helped with our stress management and our coping resources if we are to be able to parent effectively.

Toward that end I have been including a stress management module in my parent training for several decades now. The major impetus for the inclusion of this material was my own bout with a life-threatening disability. My asthma and severe allergies were the result of a genetic predisposition that killed five of my siblings and my mother. After an injection of an X-Ray dye in a hospital nearly killed me, the effects of asthma and respiratory allergies curtailed my activities more and more so that eventually I was a prisoner in my own air-filtered office and bedroom. I was on crutches from the side effects of my medications. Eventually my doctor encouraged me to examine my stress. It was intense, and I realized that unless I did something better to manage and cope with it, I was a goner. I felt I was walking a tight rope without a net.

Through daily practice, I became skilled at accessing a deeply relaxed state every morning and evening. I made several tapes for myself, often with the sounds of the ocean in the background. When I would get to that deeply relaxed place, often my grief over the many losses I'd suffered bubbled up, allowing me to cry the tears frozen deep inside where I had convinced myself I didn't have time for them.

The loss of my career as a dance teacher consumed weeks of grief resolution work. I had to accept the fact that a part of me that I had treasured was gone. I also found that when one door closed, another opened.

I used my pulse rate and my hand temperature to monitor my progress. Over the weeks and months I noticed my pulse rate was becoming slower even before the daily relaxation exercise and my hand temperature also was becoming progressively higher even before the daily relaxation. I was able to chart the reduction in my dosage and numbers of medications. Charting my progress was an enormous motivator to push me to break old habits. One year after my health crisis, my amazed doctor exclaimed, "Yvonne, I've never seen anyone with as serious a life-threatening illness turn it around as effectively as you have! Wow! Can you do this with other illnesses, too?"

"I think I can," I replied. I started to teach other patients whom he and other doctors referred to me. I taught my patients the very real mind-body connection powerful enough to reduce symptoms or cure ulcers, irritable bowel syndrome, hypertension, post traumatic stress disorder, excema, allergic dermatitis, infertility, migraines, asthma, arthritis, chronic pain, fibromyalgia, and cancer. Stress inflames tissue. Therefore if inflammation can be reduced through stress management, symptom improvement results. Depression, anxiety, and even ADHD also respond dramatically to these methods.

What causes stress? Is it the load you're carrying from the outside world: the traffic, the job, the family hassles? No, it turns out that it's none of these, it's the things we tell ourselves and we don't even know we're doing it. We stress ourselves out by the messages we send to ourselves. Our bodies respond by pumping up into overdrive as though we were about to fight off an attacker or run away from it.

Our bodies haven't changed since cave man times. Those folks who were able to stay alive long enough to produce children and stay alive long enough to raise them were the ones that were the best at becoming hyper-alert in an instant. Because there were so many environmental dangers out there, these people could move into flight/fight response very quickly. We are just like those people because we descended from them. We become like those cave men and women.

Our heart beats faster; our breathing gets rapid and shallow. Our blood pressure goes up; our digestion goes haywire. Our muscles tense up and our palms start to sweat. Our hands and feet get cold because the warm blood leaves our extremities to get the critical supply of oxygen to the brain, heart, and lungs. We can do without a toe or a finger, but not without a brain, heart, or lungs. Our bodies are gearing up to run away from danger or fight it off.

The problem is: there is no wild animal chasing us. It is the words we tell ourselves that throw us into the fight/flight syndrome and we usually don't even know we're doing it to ourselves.

There are other factors that are part of a successful stress management program including sunlight, sleep, diet, exercise, and improved communication with friends and family, but deep relaxation was the key to my being able not just to stay alive but to *thrive*. I did not follow in the footsteps of most of my family and allow death to claim my life at too young an age. I used the mind-body connection to heal physically and emotionally. I eventually was able to reclaim dance in a transformed way. I now participate in and lead sacred dance in far corners of the world.

Stress management was one of the best stepping stones to becoming a better parent. No, not just a stepping stone, stress management opened the door that had been temporarily locked to my being able to apply the parenting methods that I knew worked, but I had often been too stressed to use them. Later in my practice and for myself I put affirmations into my visualization exercises to address the deficits I found in the coping resources of parents in my patient population.

GUIDED IMAGERY

I suggest that people take their pulse rate for fifteen seconds and multiply the count by four to get a minute count. If you can find an outdoor thermometer with an exposed bulb use that, or you can use a thermistor included in the complete kit for this course, tape the thermistor to one of your fingers for a minute or two. Write down the figures for both these probes. When you finish, you'll need to write down the post treatment figures again. Next get in a relaxed posture with your spine straight either sitting or lying down. If you didn't purchase the whole *Pennington Positive Parenting* package, I recommend you put the next passage on an audio tape or CD. Look also on the website at http://www.ypsychology.com/ for free downloads!

Close your eyes, notice a slight smile on your face, and start to breathe as slowly and as deeply as you have ever done. Pay close attention to how the air fills your stomach, chest, then shoulders. Notice how your slow, even exhale almost becomes a sigh. *Ahhhh.* **Another deep breath carries you further down, down, down into a deeper level of relaxation. Each breath transports you to a more deeply relaxed place. You start to notice that with each breath you are taking in peace, calm, serenity, and tranquility. With each exhale, you breathe out all the tension, all the worries, all the anxieties. You just let go all the feelings that might be holding you back. Let them fall out of your body as you gently, slowly release the breath. You become an observer of your own breath and mark how it gently ebbs and flows just as the rhythms of your life ebb and flow.**

Imagine you're going down a flight of stairs and each step eases you down, down further into a deep, deep sanctuary of relaxation. Each of the ten steps carries you to a more deeply serene place of stillness and repose. You step down to nine. Another slow inhale and a slow exhale brings you down to eight. Another slow deep breath lowers and relaxes you further to seven. Another slow inhale and exhale eases you down to six. Another slow breath carries you down to five. Then you slowly descend to four. You see yourself float down with the breath to three. You become even more relaxed with your descent to two. Then you find yourself at the bottom with one.

You notice a door at the bottom of the stairs which opens onto the most beautiful scene you can imagine. Everywhere you look there is beauty and abundance. You step out into your favorite scene from nature, either real or imagined. A place you've visited or one you've only seen in pictures. As you look around, taking in the beauty and magic of this peaceful place, you notice that your heart is slowing down and your breathing is becoming even more relaxed and slowed down as you let go into this quiet, tranquil scene. Even the air in this place is filled with a special kind of healing light that when you breathe it in, you know deep in your bones that all is well. This magical place fills your lungs and your soul with the knowledge that you are loved and cared for. You breathe in the knowledge that you truly have everything you need right here, right now. You know deep in your

heart that you only need to be gentle with yourself and your loved ones to be totally at peace.

You find a quiet place to sit or lie down – maybe on the warm sand of a Caribbean beach, the rocking motion of a float or sail boat in azure waters of the South Pacific. Maybe you're on your back in a grassy meadow with a warm breeze and dappled sunlight on your face. You could be near a waterfall in a lush green rain forest. You can smell and hear this peaceful place all around you. Just as you find your special place, you notice all the people, real or imagined, living or dead, that have ever had your best interests at heart. These beings slowly start to form a circle around you of community and support for you. You look at their smiling faces, knowing they are sending love and encouragement to you every minute of every day. They each move forward and touch your heart, your shoulder, your hand, or your cheek sending the wordless message of love, peace, and caring to the core of your being. As you lie or sit, you know down to a soul level that the messages you are are about to hear from these precious, healing beings are your own deep, abiding truth. You listen to these words and allow them to help you. These wise, caring people – alive and well deep inside you – tell you slowly and carefully these words:

My mind and body are becoming more and more relaxed. My feet are heavy, relaxed and comfortable. My legs, torso, arms and hands are more and more relaxed. My heart is slowing further down. My breathing is slowing down. I feel warmth moving down my arms and into my hands and they are warm, warm, warm. I feel the warm sun warming my body and warming my hands so that my hands are warm and relaxed. The warmth flows down my arms and into my hands. My neck, shoulders, jaw and forehead are relaxed and smooth. My inner world is peaceful, tranquil, and   still. My mind is at ease as my muscles become more and more stretched out, heavy, loose, and limp. My heart slows down even further. It is here in my inner sanctuary that I receive these profound truths, take them into my heart, and let them help me:

> I have all the time, energy, and money I need.
> I'm perfect right now, just the way I am.
> I have all the resources I need in this moment.
> I am a good person.
> I believe in the basic goodness of others.
> My actions show love and affection daily.
> I expect and receive love and respect.
> I show my good intentions in word and deed.
> I express my feelings and needs in a caring manner.
> I am perfectly welcome anywhere I am.
> Every day in every way I embrace more peace and love.
> All of my feelings are acceptable.
> I have a right to fulfill my needs in a respectful way.

I call on the wise person inside to guide my steps.
My own wisdom and patience deep inside support me.
Anytime, anywhere I can calm myself to clarity.
I am choosing not to have to have my way.
Everything inside me is healthy, strong, and loving.
I can still be happy.
There is plenty of hope.
I am getting better at catching myself and staying on track.
My gifts to my children are love and firm boundaries.
Even if someone disapproves, I know my own worth.
I'm good at some things and that's enough.
I surround myself with positive people and attitudes.
I live in gratitude for my blessings.
I build cooperative, contributing, caring people in my family.
I return to a tranquil place daily.
My thoughts create my beautiful world.
I accept challenges as ways to grow.
I am learning to accept what I cannot change.
I am a powerful agent for change in my own life.

At this time you say goodbye to your helpers knowing you can call them back anytime you need them. You can return to the peaceful place of renewal anytime you need it. You gather yourself up from this reverie and repose and make your way back to the door to the stairs. You climb them from one to ten returning to everyday consciousness. You open your eyes and stretch, looking at the world with fresh eyes. Then find your pulse and count it. Notice your hand temperature and record it. Notice the improvement in such a short time, even though it sometimes takes a little practice to see the benefits.

You may need to add your own affirmations to the list above in the guided imagery. Circle off which of these you may need to hear and start telling yourself any of these positive statements:

I am beautiful, capable, and lovable.

I am kind and loving at my core.

I am my age and my weight.

I have much to share with the world.

I am competent and allow others to be.

I grow more attractive from the inside every day.

I am a loving and caring person and I allow others to love and care for me.

My family and I deserve the best in life.

I have much to offer and people recognize that.

I am what I do and think.

The past is behind me. I did the best I could with what I had at the time.

I love the world as it in turn loves me back.

Add your own here:

_____

_____

_____

Through the decades in my clinical practice I have noticed that when parents first arrive at my training course, they show significant symptoms of stress as measured on my own Stress/Burnout Form. The mothers – true to form – are usually more stressed than dads at the beginning.

At the end of six weeks the parents have been focusing energy on changing one behavior at a time in their children. They have concentrated on what's right about their children rather than the old way. They have used tokens as symbolic love notes to their kids delivered frequently throughout the day and all week. These tokens became markers of baby steps, later milestones toward the eventual great change in behavior the kids have soon achieved. The parents have learned to employ encouragement to motivate rather than criticism. They've become better listeners and speakers to their children. No wonder their stress profiles improve by the end of the course. You might want to rate yourself on this same scale below. Scoring is done by weighting the column titled "Never" at *0*. The "Seldom" column gets a *1*. The "Often" column scores a *2*. The "Usually/Always" column gets a *3*.

STRESS/ BURN OUT FORM © YVONNE V. PENNINGTON 1983, 2007

	Never	Seldom	Often	Usually/Always
1. General Irritability, super-sensitivity, hyper-excitation				
2. Pounding or racing heart				
3. Dryness of throat or mouth				
4. Impulsive behavior, emotional instability				
5. Urge to run, cry, or hide				
6. Poor concentration				
7. Feelings of unreality, weakness, or dizziness				
8. Tendency to become fatigued				
9. Floating anxiety, feeling vaguely worried				
10. Emotional tension, hyper-alertness, feeling "keyed up"				
11. Trembling, nervous tics				
12. Tendency to be easily startled				
13. High pitched or nervous laughter				
14. Stuttering or other speech difficulties				
15. Grinding or clinching teeth				
16. Insomnia or more than usual amount of sleep				
17. Restlessness, inability to sit quietly and relax				
18. More than usual sweating (palms or elsewhere)				
19. Frequent need to urinate, bed wetting				
20. Diarrhea, constipation, queasiness, vomiting, indigestion,				
21. Headaches, stomaches, other aches and pains				
22. Pain or tightness in neck, shoulders, lower back				
23. Loss of or excessive appetite, excessive weight loss or gain				
24. Smoking				
25. Increased use of legally prescribed drugs:tranquilizers, sleep meds				
26. Increased use of alcohol or drug use including sugar, caffeine				
27. Nightmares or disturbing dreams				
28. Suspicious, inflexible or compulsive thoughts or behavior				
29. Withdrawal from social contact				
30. Accident proneness				
31. Cold hands and/or feet				
33. Feeling sad, depressed				
34. Bored, loss of interest in work, hobbies, play, sex				
35. Short, irregular, or shallow breathing				
36. Tightly gripping chair arm or steering wheel				
37. Popping jaw, knuckles				
38. Frowning, squinting				
39. "Butterflies" in stomach				
40. Inability to make decision				
41. Forgetfulness				

If your score is below 10, you are in great shape. If your score is in the teens you are about average for parents of ADHD children. If your score is higher, you owe it to yourself and your family to do something about managing your stress response. You often cannot change the stressful events in your life, but you can change how you view them and respond to them. If there are stressful situations or people in your life, try to make changes for the better in those environments. You may have to take a short or longer break from friends or family members that seem toxic to your well being. By all means use the suggestions in this course to improve your ability to handle things. If you cannot do it alone, get some help from a local mental health professional. Be sure and reward yourself for sticking to a well designed self improvement project.

Way back in the seventies, two researchers, Holmes and Rahe, at the University of Washington Medical School, interviewed more than a thousand heart patients for the amount of life changes they had undergone in the past year. They found that the best predictor of extremely serious health crises was the amount of life changes – good and bad – the person had undergone in a relatively short time. They assigned a point value to each event, calling it the Life Changes Scale, thereby becoming able to predict major emotional or physical breakdowns with amazing accuracy.

Dr. Yamamoto, a psychologist at the University of Arizona, queried 367 fourth-, fifth-, and sixth-graders about how worried they would be about different events. Losing a parent and going blind were deemed the worst and about equal in producing anxiety according to these kids. Next came being held back a grade, wetting your pants in class, and hearing your parents quarrel, being seen as about equally stressful. The children rated being caught stealing, being suspected of lying, and receiving a bad report card were the next down in ratings for worrisome events. They rated being sent to the principal's office, having an operation, and getting lost as about the same in stress perception. Next came being made fun of in class, moving to a new school, and having a scary dream in ranking. Not making a 100 on a test, being picked last for a team, and losing at a game were viewed about the same and only mildly troublesome. Last came the dentist, giving a report in class, and getting a new sibling. Until this study many of us had viewed the birth of a sibling as much more stressful than the kids view it themselves.

So when we apply the idea to children that they can become stressed out, too, we find they need some stress management, also. Indeed we are finding that stress exacerbates almost any condition or illness in children and adults. Dr. David Elkins noted how stressful life events could pile up on your child, just as with adults. . The more changes she experiences in a short time – say a year - the more likely she is to have health or behavioral difficulties. We could assign a point value similar to Holmes and Rahe or we could ask children to assign the point values, themselves, as I do in my office. I start with a parent dying as the most stressful event imaginable in a child's life and ask the kids to take it from there. Do this interview with your child for a real eye opener. Write down the numerical response when you ask your child, " How stressful for you would be the following events from 1 to 100?"

Parental death	100
Parental divorce	___
Parental separation	___
Parental travel in career	___
Close family member dies	___

Personal illness/injury ___

Parent remarries ___

Parent fired from job ___

Parents reconcile ___

Parents quarrel ___

Parent returns to work ___

Health change for family member ___

Mother becomes pregnant ___

School difficulties ___
 (range of severity 39-50 maybe, add points for each additional day of difficulty)

Bad report card ___

Sent to principal or suspended ___

Birth of sibling ___

School adjustment ___
 (new teacher, new class, Spec. Ed. entrance, removal)

Change in family finances ___

Injury/ illness of close friend ___

Death of friend/ school mate ___

New or change in extracurricular ___

 activities (Scouts, music, sports,etc)

Change in number of sibling fights ___

Threat of violence at school ___

Theft of possessions ___

Change in responsibilities at home ___

Older sibling leaves home ___

Trouble with grandparents
    or extended family ___

Outstanding personal achievement ___

Move to another city, part of town ___

Receiving/losing pet ___

Change in personal habits ___

Trouble with teacher ___

Change in hours with
    sitter or day care ___

Move to new house ___

Start new school ___

Test you didn't study for ___

Change in play habits ___

Vacation with family ___

Changes in friends ___

Attending summer camp ___

Change in sleeping habits ___

Change in amount of
    screen time ___

Birthday party ___

Punished for not telling the truth ___

According to Holmes and Rahe for adults, a score of 300 or more holds a better than fifty percent probability that some major behavioral or health issue will occur. Adults get really stressed out from life changes. So do kids. Would you say that your child is stressed?

Do you stop vacations, summer camp, family moves, or requiring more chores with advances in age? Of course not. Good adjustment results from facing life's challenges and surmounting them, not living in a stress-free bubble. If we can manage our stress we can deal with our kids and spouses from a more relaxed, centered place. If we can teach our kids to manage their stress, they can tackle life's hurdles much more easily.

Sunlight, play, hugs, good nutrition, exercise, thoughts that promote health and happiness, a supportive environment that reminds us of our strengths daily, being able to share our feelings with someone, and getting to a deep place of relaxation daily are critical components of a healthy lifestyle that offers inoculation from the effects of stress. Adequate sleep is a big part of stress management. The way you know you and your youngster are getting enough sleep is that you wake up in the morning without an alarm or someone waking you. How may of these health promoting behaviors are you doing? List them here.

_____

_____

_____

_____

A study by Dornbusch at Stanford years ago on almost 8,000 high school students found that parents getting upset about bad grades only served to make marks decline even further. Punishment also didn't work to improve things. Remember the young person is probably already stressed out about the low marks. What worked to get better grades was low key praise.

This is not praise that is laid on too thick, not truthful or insincere. The praise is generally not about the overall person of the teen, "You're such an angel." Instead it is praise that is specific to the particular behavior at hand. It is honest and heartfelt. Finding something to appreciate and praise in the current behavior and effort of the youngster is worth all the punishment and criticism one can possibly pile on. Dornbusch also found encouragement and offers to help brought about improved school grades, too.

So what do you do as a parent when your child's grades are going downhill and underneath it all, you are sure it's all your fault and you're a poor excuse for a parent? First, you do a bit of stress management on yourself so you can tackle this from a loving and patient place. You watch your diet, you talk to yourself that this is not the end of the world. You take a break and do something fun. You review the affirmations you really need to hear often from the guided imagery in this chapter. You take a walk, get some sleep, get to a deeply relaxed place using the guided imagery in this book. Do this guided imagery daily, not just when you feeling stressed.

Then when you are at a good place yourself, you search out anything positive you can say about that report card and recent behaviors and effort from the teen that might have been attempts to bring up the marks. You do not concentrate just on the bad grades. That's the old way and you now know better. You use <u>I-Messages</u> to convey your feelings underneath your anger that he's been totally goofing off. You convey your worry about his future and the guilt that you've not been available enough to help. You ask the child to make a plan for improving things while you **really listen** to any good points the child makes that could ameliorate the situation. You and the child write out a contingency contract for improvement. You arrange a time when you check in with each other in a few days to see how well it's working. You arrange to get daily feedback from the teacher as to how well the child is managing his assignments and his time. If he's been lying about homework to get out of the work, he has to do a <u>Real Apology</u> to mend the parent-child relationship and start to rebuild your trust. If he refuses, he must stay in his room until he complies, because he must get as real and authentic as you are now with him.

When kids and adults are stressed we tend to show our anger to the people we are around most. The problem is that anger is almost always a secondary emotion. Getting mad and screaming at your family members rarely solves anything. There is much more underneath the anger. It's like a big old iceberg. We can see the anger and show it, but all the other feelings of the iceberg are invisible, below the water line in the iceberg. Usually we are not even aware, ourselves, of the feelings underneath the anger. It takes some work to ferret out the primary feelings, but it's worth it.

Why are we so mad? It's usually because we are hurt or worried. If we can talk to our spouses and our kids about how their behavior affects us rather than what's wrong with the other person, we are well on our way to having kids listen to us rather than become "parent deaf" We need to share with our kids the pain, guilt, disappointment, and fear that drives our anger and they will be more able to listen and work with us on a way to change things.

Here are some events and the typical angry "you" responses parents are likely to make. See if you can find the real feeling underneath the anger iceberg:

EVENT	ANGRY RESPONSE	REAL FEELING
Daughter hours late getting home.	*"You're grounded. I'm furious."*	Fear
Child acts up in store	*"Just wait till I get you home."*	Embarrassment
D's and F's on report card	*"You've been goofing off."*	Worry, sadness, guilt
Child's belongings strewn	*"You expect me to be the maid."*	_____
Husband forgets anniversary	*"You're thoughtless."*	_____

The next time you're feeling angry at your child, see if you can share the real feelings underneath the anger iceberg with your child and ask for change in the form of an <u>I-Message</u>.

Poor stress management is an enormous contributor to family strife. Waiting for other members of your family to manage their stress before you get around to managing yours is not going to work. It's up to you to present the calm amidst the chaos.

I heard a story about the bombing in Sarajevo. Dozens of ordinary citizens – children, pregnant women, elderly men – were lined up at a bakery to buy bread and other baked goods one bright sunny day. Bombers flew over, dropping their deadly cargo annihilating everyone. A cellist with the symphony lived across the street and saw the horror. The next day he dressed in his tails, brought a chair and played all day on the ruins of that bakery. The bombing continued. People stopped to ask him "How can you play your music when there is bombing here?" The gentle cellist queried, "How can they bomb here while I play my music?"

You can be that quiet center of peace amidst the anger and chaos in the household. By choosing to control your emotions to get to serenity and tranquility, amazing things can happen. Decisions made that are really good and sure and just are made from a place deep inside of quiet and calm.

Review, Homework and Application of Chapter 9

1. Make a tape of the relaxation exercise in this chapter or use to DVD of Session 6 of the live workshop. Use it daily and chart your progress by rating your stress level on my Stress/ Burnout form. Also take your pulse rate and your hand temperature before and after you do the exercise. Maybe you could give yourself some points for improvement in your physiological probes and points for sticking to you program. Chart your progress on one of the charts in this book.

2. Write the affirmations you most need to tell yourself from the list in this chapter or things you know yourself you really need to hear.

   _____

   _____

   _____

   _____

3. Compose an "<u>I-Message</u>" about a child not cleaning up after making a snack and leaving the kitchen a mess. This is an alternative to the screaming, yelling, or resentful seething we parents slip into that is so stressful to ourselves and our children.

   When you <u>leave the kitchen a mess after making a snack.</u>

   I feel _____(don't talk about how angry or frustrated you are or use the words "like" of "that"

   I need_____.

   Will you _____?

   If you will, I will _____.

218

4. Write you stress management plan here:

   a. I will increase my level of exercise to ____ minutes this week.

   b. I will increase my level of sunlight to ____ hours a day (Ideal is 2 hours).

   c. I will reduce sugar, white flour, and hydrogenated fats in my diet this week by
   _____.

   d. I will ensure that I get seven to eight hours sleep nightly by_____.

   e. I will practice <u>I-Message</u> and reflective listening with family members to improve communication by _____.

   f. I will get to a deeply relaxed state of meditation, visualization, or prayer at least _____minutes daily/weekly.

   g. I will use a plan to improve the things I can, but learn to let go or _____ the things I can't.

   h. I will make sure I build in some fun and time for myself daily by
   _____.

6. Divide a blank sheet of paper in half. On the left side list the behaviors and characteristics you wanted in your child before he/she was born. On the other side of the paper, list the characteristics and behaviors that you got in your child. At the bottom of the page, grade yourself – A,B,C, D, or F – on how well you've come to terms with the difference.

7. Make sure you put some fun in your life by _____.

8. Continue your behavior modification project, chart it, call a friend for support.

9. Make a written plan to keep these changes going six months from now.

ANSWERS: Completely up to you. Reread them and see if they make sense to you.

CHAPTER NINE

MY PLAN FOR IMPROVEMENT

My plan to exhibit more leadership and ultimate goal orientation of good adult outcome with my family is_____.

I will know it's working when_____.

I plan to do less of these (Circle all that apply.): put downs, discouragement, losing my temper, being impatient, belittling and being inconsiderate, staying disconnected from my feelings and the feelings of my family, etc,_____

I plan to do more of these (circle all that apply.) showing unconditional love and acceptance, offering help, understanding my stress and that of my family, improving my coping resources for stress management, finding time for fun, collaborating, reaching out, forgiving myself and family, listening with a third ear, etc,

_____

The specifics of my plan are:

Monday_____

Tuesday_____

Wednesday_____

Thursday_____

Friday_____

Saturday_____

Sunday_____

Complete this page, photocopy it, and carry it with you daily.

CHAPTER 10

WHAT TO DO TILL THE PSYCHOLOGIST COMES

Dr. Barkin at Vanderbilt Children's Hospital in Nashville did a study on child discipline recently on more than 2000 parents of children ages two to eleven. She found that forty-five percent of parents use Time Out, forty- two percent of parents claimed to use removal of privileges. Thirteen percent admit to yelling at their children. Nine percent confess to spanking. I think the prevalence of yelling and spanking is much higher. It's just that parents are too ashamed to admit it. Most parents reported their methods not working very well - any of them. They report using the same methods used by their parents even though the methods were ineffective. None report the use of positive discipline techniques. None, zilch, nada! Lots of work to do here.

If you can't take two aspirin and call me in the morning and you can't attend one of my workshops or retreats and a problem behavior continues to occur, ask yourself these questions: Is it so disruptive, you can't continue? Is it so habitual, repetitive, or so bizarre as to inhibit the child's learning or social interaction? Is it dangerous to the child or others? If the answer to each question is "No," then ignore it for a while and see if it doesn't go away. If it doesn't stop, try these next ideas. Concentrate on positive techniques at first unless the behavior is dangerous or illegal.

Positive Management Techniques for Disruptive, Inappropriate Mal-adaptive, Habitual, and/or Non-cooperative Behaviors

1. Reinforce other children and adults for ignoring off task behavior.

2. Reinforce the target child more often for the incompatible behavior.

3. Reinforce other children for the incompatible behavior more often.

4. Use a timer for small time allotments.

5. Reduce the time the child is expected to participate in a task before he is reinforced.

6. Give more positive reinforcement, stronger and more valuable activity reinforcement, more frequent token reinforcement. Pair token reinforcement more often with praise. Incentives are good motivators for adults and children.

7. Check for reinforcer satiation. She could be tired of candy, playing ball, or just not interested any more.

8. Enclose or screen off distractions for the target child or group so that other children cannot see the off-task child. Eliminate tempting environment.

9. Reduce the difficulty of the expected task. Make sure the learning material is at his mastery level. Make more easy requests to get compliance jump started. Prime the pump.

10. Go back to where he had been successful, then gradually increase the level of complexity again in smaller steps this time.

11. Change the triggering stimulus that precedes the undesirable behavior. Then gradually work the stimulus back in. Use prevention, not punishment if it can be avoided.

12. Use praise that is uncontaminated. Don't add a zinger at the end when you give him a compliment. Remember USHIC: Uncontaminated, specific, honest, immediate, and consistent.

13. Find out if other factors could be contributing to the unacceptable behavior. Could she be frightened, worried, threatened, stressed? Consultation may be necessary.

14. There may be a limited personal relationship between the child and parent or teacher. More bonding and doing fun things together may be needed.

15. Child may be getting reinforcement non-contingently by manipulation. Out smart him.

16. Child's self esteem may be so low she undermines her own success. Make sure praise is USHIC. Involve in fun activities in which she can be successful.

17. If the child is too depressed to accept rewards or praise, get professional help.

18. Observe the child to find out what might motivate him.

19. There is little investment from the child. Do <u>I-Message</u>, family meeting, written contingency contracting.

Negative Control Techniques if the Behavior is Dangerous, Defiant, Violent to Objects or People, or Against the Laws of Society

1. Use all the positive techniques first. Be sure you are reinforcing the opposite or incompatible behavior very frequently, if you plan to punish.

2. For dangerous or violent behavior, use an immediate punisher: Time Out for children under twelve, or time in the child's room as well as grounding (loss of all privileges) for older children. It doesn't matter so much the length of Time Out, but the consistency and immediacy. For older children use logical and natural consequences. Younger children respond to natural consequences, too.

3. Train Time Out behavior by using the laundry room or bathroom as back up if the child refuses to stay in the Time Out chair in the corner.

4. In the car use Time Out by forcing the child's head between his knees for the appropriate time. Use a warning first.

5. In public find the nearest corner of the store and have the child face the corner for the correct amount of time. No one looks at the child nor talks to the child.

6. Take away a positive reinforcement such as a privilege or a token. Fine only once or twice, then isolate the youngster. Make sure he has a way to earn back his privilege or his tokens.

7. Ignore temper outbursts in Time Out. Be calm.

8. Aggression on the way to Time Out earns more time in isolation.

9. If property is damaged in Time Out, *overcorrection* is used.

10. If the behavior is against the rules of society: lying, cheating, drugging, stealing,

defiance of authority, threatening, or violence, a **Real Apology** must take place to all the victims involved, especially to the parents who suffer disappointment, worry, pain, and embarrassment from such behavior. The youngster must stay in her room until the written apology is finished. She is only allowed out for school, meals, and bathroom. The acts that make up the making amends part of the apology must be accomplished without complaining, reminding, or whining, otherwise the child must return to her room and develop in writing further chores to do to make amends. The plan to make sure the same behavior doesn't happen again must be specific and written.

11. Be consistent and immediate with punishment.
12. If the behavior does not decrease, consultation is needed.

How to Convince a Teacher to Try Your Proven Methods

Teachers sometimes have arguments against using operant conditioning techniques. An excellent way to counteract some of a teacher's objections is to take your pre-treatment and post-treatment charts with you for scientific proof of the efficacy of operant conditioning. Remember that teachers choose teaching because of their commitment and because they wanted to make a difference. They're certainly not in it for the money. Remind yourself and her of the reasons that brought her here. She wanted to see children achieve in school and life.

Here are some of the more common objections to helping your child. Included are some response you can make to these objections.

Teacher 1: The point system is giving special treatment to just one child. It's not fair. The other kids will resent it and make trouble. He'll feel different.

Parent: We all want to treat children equally if possible, but children come to us at all different ability level so that it is impossible to treat everyone absolutely equally. Giving them different grades is unequal.

When we punish, we single kids out. When we give grades, we give different grades. We individualize academic work to a child's ability. Academic work, why not behavior change learning? Adults are paid different amounts in their pay all in the same room. I don't know of very many adults that work without pay or incentives. For kids who have no pay off for good behavior, it is expecting too great a leap for them to do it without some reward. What if I rewarded his behavior at home for daily feedback slips from you?

Teacher 2: I feel his problems are more deep seated than this. If we deal just with his temper tantrums, his emotional problems will just come out in worse ways. You're just treating the symptoms, not the real problem.

Parent: You may be right that his problems may be deep seated. They may go all the way back to his early childhood, but we don't have the skills to take him back to his early childhood and help him through his childhood again. Research has shown that the opposite is true for symptom substitution in that as a person gets better in one part of his life he'll usually have a spillover and improve in other parts of his life, too. We must deal with his behavior now, and he must stop his tantrums if he is to function in society.

Teacher 3: All these points and tokens make it seem like the kids are all robots or in the Army or something. Everybody lines up and gets his points. I don't like it.

Parent: We can individualize it more for each child, but that will take a lot more work from you. Nobody works at a task without being motivated. If the kid will work and learn new behaviors without points, he doesn't need them. If he can't change his behavior without incentives, it's up to us to provide the necessary reinforcement. Let me show you the chart we made to show Johnny's improvement at home. He loves it and he doesn't feel like he is a robot or in the Army at all.

Teacher 4: This behavior modification is for the birds. It's too much work for one kid and neglecting all the rest of them. I think he ought to be in a special class where they have special techniques.

Parent: Setting up a program is a tremendous amount of work; after it gets going, it almost runs itself. There is a lot of time and effort involved, but right now a lot of time and effort is being expended in punishing him and in trying to get him on task with methods that just aren't working. For just a small amount more effort, we can use something that works for a change and is much, much more pleasant to use for you, the principal, the other kids, and my child. In a special class they'd use exactly these techniques; sometimes a special class worsens a child's condition because he loses normal peers to model good behavior for him. Don't you think it's worth the effort for something that we know will work?

Teacher 5: This is bribery. These kids ought to learn without candy and games. If we pay them to learn, they'll always expect to get paid to do things.

Parent: Have one of these brownies I baked for you because I know what a handful my child can be and I really appreciate your extra work. With adults (including teachers for a pay raises and graduate credit) and kids, if incentives aren't offered to learn new behavior, the learning simply does not take place. Bribery is paying someone to do something immoral or illegal. We are not asking the child to do anything like that.

Teacher 6: This is way too much work to do this. I don't get paid for all this extra work.

Parent: You are so right. Teachers are paid way too little for all they do. This is a lot of work. Perhaps we need to set up an Individual Education Plan to more carefully describe his needs in the regular classroom and the Section 504 accommodations required in the regular class for his disability of ADHD (or other disorder). Maybe we can get you some help if we put the formal plan in writing. How do I go about requesting such an IEP meeting?

How to Choose Which Method to Use

So far in our journey through effective methods to change behavior in our children and ourselves, we have covered contingency contracting, removal of attention, token economies, logical and natural consequences, response cost in the form of grounding or other loss of tokens or privileges, Time Out, training Time Out, reflective listening, I-Messages, brainstorming, stress management, deep relaxation, guided imagery, appreciation exercises, aerobic exercise, Omega 3, USHIC praise, extra bonding and fun time, enriching the positive reinforcement schedule, using a **Real Apology**, and affirmations. We covered family meetings. We also covered *over correction*. It depends on who owns the problem as to which method to use. We know by now that to keep a behavior going, we must switch to intermittent reinforcement.

Most problems are no big deals in families. What the child wears as long as certain body parts are covered and what she eats as long as she is not starving herself are typical examples of no-contest issues. The rest sometimes involve some action to change things. The person who owns the problem is the person most likely to seek help in solving the problem. So you see, most of parenting problems are owned by the parent. Usually the kids doesn't care if his chores ever get done. He's okay to sleep till noon and stay up all night. The teen isn't worried about getting in after curfew unless she's caught. So if the child owns the problem, reflective listening is suggested then brainstorming. Otherwise all the other methods are possibilities for parents to use.

By the end of this course I usually ask the parents themselves to decide which interventions to use for each problem. You try these:

PROBLEM	WHO OWNS IT	INTERVENTION
Child won't sleep in own bed	*parent*	I-message, relaxation education, token economy, removal of attention for inappropriate behavior
Child can't get along with siblings	*parent*	Token economy reinforcing good sibling behavior
Temper tantrums	_____	_____
Dawdling	_____	_____
Child complains no one likes him	_____	_____
Child steals food and lies about it	_____	_____

For tantrums, I hope you answered that it's the parent's problem and ignoring it by leaving the room is the best strategy. Dawdling is also the parent's problem and best handled by a token economy and logical and natural consequences. If your child complains no one likes him, it's his problem and the parent needs to use reflective listening. Then some brainstorming would be a good idea. You need to help him find out is he is doing anything that puts other kids off. If the problem persists and becomes chronic, professional help may be needed to enhance his social skills. Stealing and lying are problems owned by parents because the child has no investment in changing. A Real Apology is a necessary first step and he stays in his room until the whole thing is written and read to the victim. Logical and natural consequences could include loss of kitchen privileges for a day or a meal for stealing and lying.

230

PARENTS ACHIEVE LASTING CHANGES IN CHILDREN BY CHANGING THEIR OWN BEHAVIOR

At the end of this course most parents have gotten to a pretty good place in their relationship with their children. They have been able to take these ideas and apply them well and make informed, goal-directed decisions that improve their behavior as well as the behavior of the whole family.

They've been able to take hypothetical situations and design and appropriate intervention for each problem. In their own lives they have a new sense of self confidence as do their children.

At the end of the course I ask parents to come up with mottoes for what they've learned and what they plan to remember to do.

Here are some examples:

Accentuate the positive.

If you want something to grow, water it.

If I want someone to change, I must change first.

If the behavior doesn't change, it's a bad program not a bad child.

Add your own here: _____

_____

_____

ABC'S OF CHILD MANAGEMENT

Accentuate the positive. **Applaud** success rather than belaboring failure.

Behavior is learned. It can be unlearned and replaced by new and appropriate behaviors.

Consistency brings about security and behavior change. **Conflict** between parents will undermine discipline faster than anything. Logical and natural **consequences** must be experienced by the child for misbehavior to be eliminated. After the new behavior is established, intermittently reinforce.

Don't attack the personality. Separate the behavior from the child.

Encouragement is necessary. The child and you must believe she can succeed.

Forget past transgressions. Once punishment has taken place, the slate is wiped clean.

Good behavior should be noticed and praised. Catch the child being good and describe to the child what specific behavior he did that you appreciate. Let him overhear you complimenting him to relatives.

Help him meet the goals you both set. Don't wait for him to be national champion before he hears a word of praise. Show appreciation for small steps along the way.

Interrogation is not successful. He doesn't know why he did it. Have him repeat the rule he broke and administer the consequence. Be **immediate** with positive reinforcement and punishment.

Judgment, criticism and comparison to other children and siblings demoralize a child and make her want to give up. If she's overly afraid of making errors, she cannot do her best.

Kindness: Remember that discipline is to teach and train the child, not to get even with him. Don't turn praise into an unkind statement: "You can be so nice, when you want to be."

Limits: Children must know that certain behaviors are not acceptable. There must be certain behaviors that are non-negotiable. They usually include lying, stealing, cheating, hitting, misuse or destruction of property, and defiance. Immediate and consistent punishment are needed for these.

Model appropriate behavior. So many times we don't mean what we say or say what we mean. The child knows that the truth lies in the behavior, If you tell your child not to smoke between puffs of a cigarette, which message will he hear?

Negotiate: Many behaviors can be negotiated. If the child is allowed some control over part of his life, he will feel less need to demand control over others.

Opportunity: Give your child the opportunity to have a feeling of success by allowing him to have responsibility for household chores.

Positive: Become very aware if how few positive you tell your child and set about increasing these.

Quest: View parenting as a never ending quest in training children in values, attitudes, and behaviors that are cooperative and contributing. Good management involves getting people to do what you want without threatening or hitting them. Apply such techniques with your child.

Remove the pay off for the misbehavior (It is usually attention.), and the misbehavior will decrease or disappear.

State the household rules simply and positively. Keep them brief and under six in number. Written rules posted with consequences in the kitchen are extremely useful.

Threats don't work. Remember they're almost impossible to carry out. Make the punishment fit the crime. Don't say depreciative things such as, "You'll be the death of me."

Utilize natural reinforcers occurring in the everyday environment: "You did such a good job getting to dinner on time, you get to choose family dessert."

Verbalize your appreciation for little things. Your spouse and your child need to hear it.

Work: A low frequency behavior (work) will increase if followed by a high frequency behavior (play). Make it a household rule that first we work, then we play.

EXamine the areas of frustration and stress in you life. Children are often targets for displaced anger. Is your child bearing the brunt of your frustration with yourself, your boss, or your spouse?

You: It really is up to you. You can change your child's behavior and his destiny in spite of the fact that parenting is the hardest job there is, and few parents have any good training for it.

Zero in on one behavior at a time. Don't try to change all the child's negative behavior at once Behavior change in small, measured doses really is very successful.

CHAPTER TEN

MY PLAN FOR IMPROVEMENT

My plan to improve my mentorship and advocacy for my family and others is _____.

I will know it's working when_____.

I plan to do less of these (Circle all that apply.): withdraw, distrust, blame, angry messages, etc, _____.

I plan to do more of these (Circle all that apply.): engage, be emotionally available, reflective listening, motivate, praise without contamination, use I-messages, use patience, hugs, positive behavior change project, switch to intermittent reinforcement, etc, _____.

The specifics are these:

Monday_____

Tuesday_____

Wednesday_____

Thursday_____

Friday_____

Saturday_____

Sunday_____

Complete this page, photocopy it, and carry it with you daily.

Dr, Yvonne Pennington is a child and adult psychologist, marriage and family therapist, registered play therapist and supervisor, and certified Sandplay Therapist, Teaching Member ISST. She has been in the mental health field for thirty-six years, presenting frequently at local, state, regional, national and international conferences. She has served on the Board of Learning Disabilities Association of Georgia, the Georgia Governor's Advisory Panel for Educational Needs of Handicapped Children, and is currently on the Professional Advisory Board of CHADD chapters for Cobb, Cherokee, and North Atlanta, GA. Former Director of the ground-breaking Northside Child Development Institute at Northside Hospital, specializing in ADHD and other learning disabilities, Dr. Pennington offers evaluation, group, family and individual therapy in her Marietta and Atlanta offices. She has been offering effective, research-based parent training as part of a comprehensive treatment package for her full career. Her parent training for ADHD kids consistently rivals medication in effectiveness. She holds diplomates in psychotherapy and sports psychology. She is the author of the E-book, "School Survival Skills" and the soon to be released e-books: "Personal Best Club: A Social Skills Workbook", "Raising Amazing Kids: Parenting Successful Offspring, Even if One Has ADHD" and the DVD *Pennington Positive Parenting.* . She enjoys hosting retreats in soul-soothing places such as Bali and her Full Circle Retreat Center in Marietta GA. She also loves dance and spending time with her family, especially her two grown sons. They are Wynn Pennington, owner of MOTOVINO wines in 27 states, and Ty Pennington, star of the hit ABC show, Extreme Makeover Home Edition, who also has ADHD. She is available at www.ypsychology.com and www.yvpennington.com.